Woody Allen

Woody Allen

*An Essay on the Nature
of the Comical*

VITTORIO HÖSLE

University of Notre Dame Press
Notre Dame, Indiana

Library of Congress Cataloging-in-Publication Data

Hösle, Vittorio, 1960–
    Woody Allen : an essay on the nature of the comical / Vittorio Hösle.
        p.   cm.
    Includes index.
    ISBN-13: 978-0-268-03104-6 (pbk. : alk. paper)
    ISBN-10: 0-268-03104-5 (pbk. : alk. paper)
    1. Allen, Woody—Criticism and interpretation.   2. Comic, The.   I. Title.
    PN1998.3.A45H67   2007
    791.43'092—dc22
                                                    2007003386

∞ *The paper in this book meets the guidelines for permanence and durability*
of the Committee on Production Guidelines for Book Longevity of
the Council on Library Resources.

For Jieon, Johannes, and Paul,
the counterworld to Woody Allen

Contents

Preface to the
English Book Version

This little book was published first in English in the journal *Film and Philosophy,* which in 2000 dedicated a special issue, edited by Sander Lee, to Woody Allen, who turned sixty-five in that year. It owes much to discussions with my wife, Jieon Kim, and my friend Mark Roche, who was kind enough to go through this text and suggest linguistic and substantive improvements. I then translated it into German, and it was published in hardcover in 2001 by C. H. Beck and in paperback by Deutscher Taschenbuch Verlag in 2005 on the occasion of Allen's seventieth birthday. The Spanish edition with Tusquets came out in 2002.

The numerous reviews of the book that appeared in German, Austrian, Swiss, Swedish, Icelandic, Mexican, Argentine, and Chilean newspapers and journals have encouraged me to present it also to an English-speaking public as a little monograph, even if I am aware of two of its shortcomings. First, it is written by a European, whose view of Allen will be necessarily different from that of an American. Second, it is written by a philosopher, not a film studies professor. These two limitations, however, may also have some benefits attached to them. First, it is not accidental that Allen's films have been a greater success in Europe than in the United States; there is a specific intellectuality in his humor that particularly the American Midwest does not seem to enjoy as much as European countries—a point made by Allen himself at the end of *Hollywood Ending* when Val Waxman, the character played by him, leaves for Europe, where his new film, which he has directed in a state of psychologically caused blindness, has become a great success. Second, the whole point of my book is that Allen is a profoundly philosophical comedian. I do not deny that he is influenced by authors like Bob Hope or the Marx Brothers; he obviously is. But it is not these influences that interest me, because my focus is on the philosophical dimension of his jokes and comical situations; and it is this dimension that raises his work so much over the comedies of his American predecessors and allows us to see in him a comedian of the same intellectual rank as Aristophanes or Molière. My essay aims at being both a new reflection on the nature of the comical and an analysis of unique features of Allen's comical universe; the development of general categories is the basis of, and is enriched by, concrete interpretations. The philosophically sophisticated reader will recognize the main sources of my approach to the comical to be Hegel, Schopenhauer, and Bergson—Hegel's intellectualism is in fact the driving force in my revision of Bergson's peerless book on laughter.

My 2000 essay was copyedited, and some passages were added that relate to some of Allen's newer films. (I thank an anonymous reviewer of Notre Dame Press for excellent suggestions.) But the core of my book is formed by Allen's movies up to the late 1990s, since the basic patterns and motives of his humor can be found there, probably in an aesthetically more compelling way than in the later works.

Woody Allen

Woody Allen

An Essay on the Nature of the Comical

Earnestness sees through the comic, and the deeper down from which it fetches itself up, the better, but it does not mediate. What earnestness wills in earnest it does not regard as comic insofar as it itself wills it, but for that reason it can readily see the comic therein. In this way the comic purifies the pathos-filled emotions, and conversely the pathos-filled emotions give substance to the comic. For example, the most devastating comic perception would be the one in which indignation is latent—yet no one detects it because of the laughter. Vis comica *[Comic power] is the most responsible weapon and thus is essentially present only in the hands of someone who has a fully equivalent pathos. Hence, anyone who could in truth make a hypocrite a butt of laughter will also be able to crush him with indignation. But anyone who wants to use indignation and does not have the corresponding* vis comica *will readily degenerate into rhetoric and will himself become comic.*

Kierkegaard, *Stages on Life's Way*, "Guilty?"/
"Not Guilty?" June 7, Midnight

1

Woody Allen is a challenge for philosophy. Why? Laughter is of course not one of the most fundamental but is nevertheless one of the most controversial and intriguing topics in philosophy, in whose analysis various philosophical disciplines have to work together—philosophical anthropology, philosophical sociology, and aesthetics proper. This bestows on comedians a certain philosophical interest—the more so since, "while comedy may be the most widely appreciated art, it is also the most undervalued,"[1] an injustice that calls for redress by philosophy. Philosophers have to operate with abstract concepts; but it is reality, or at least a certain interpretation of reality, that has to show whether the concepts developed are fruitful. Therefore, every philosopher interested in elaborating a general theory of laughter is well advised to study those works that make people laugh, and Woody Allen can claim to make a certain type of people in the late twentieth and early twenty-first centuries (mainly Western, particularly European intellectuals) laugh as nobody else can. It may well be that a careful analysis of his work will contribute to an improvement of the main theories of the comic developed till now. What are the causes of Allen's success?

First, Woody Allen has succeeded in impersonating a certain type of comic hero, and it well befits philosophy to try to find the general features common to Victor Shakapopolis in *What's New, Pussycat?*, Jimmy Bond in *Casino Royale*, Virgil Starkwell in *Take the Money and Run*, Fielding Mellish in *Bananas*, Allan Felix in *Play It Again, Sam*, the jester Felix, Fabrizio, Victor Shakapopolis again, and the loquacious and fearful sperm in *Everything You Always Wanted to Know about Sex (But Were Afraid to Ask)*, Miles

Monroe in *Sleeper,* Boris Grushenko in *Love and Death,* Alvy Singer in *Annie Hall,* Isaac Davis in *Manhattan,* Sandy Bates in *Stardust Memories,* Andrew Hobbes in *A Midsummer Night's Sex Comedy,* Leonard Zelig in *Zelig,* Danny Rose in *Broadway Danny Rose,* Mickey Sachs in *Hannah and Her Sisters,* Sheldon Mills in *Oedipus Wrecks,* Cliff Stern in *Crimes and Misdemeanors,* Nick Fifer in *Scenes from a Mall,* Max Kleinman in *Shadows and Fog,* Gabe Roth in *Husbands and Wives,* Larry Lipton in *Manhattan Murder Mystery,* Lenny Winerib in *Mighty Aphrodite,* Joe Berlin in the musical-like *Everyone Says I Love You,* Harry Block in *Deconstructing Harry,* Ray Winkler in *Small Time Crooks,* CW Briggs in *The Curse of the Jade Scorpion,* Val Waxman in *Hollywood Ending,* David Dobel in *Anything Else,* Sid Waterman in *Scoop*—and even to those persons in some of the films directed by Allen whom he did not play himself but who nevertheless share some of the aura of the comic hero usually represented by him: Kenneth Branagh in *Celebrity,* for example, plays Lee Simon in a Woody Allen-like manner (to name only one feature, he stammers). Obviously, there are huge differences between, to name only two, Victor Shakapopolis and Harry Block; however, that they have something in common is due not only to the fact that Allen's repertoire as an actor is quite restricted (therefore Block seems less mean than probably was originally intended) but even more to the desire of his public to recognize in the roles he plays something of what they associate with the Woody Allen persona—who, owing to Stuart Hample, for some years even became a cartoon character. Even if Allen were able to play a figure like Judah Rosenthal in *Crimes and Misdemeanors* or Chris Wilton in *Match Point* convincingly, his audience would be frustrated—whereas the public was perhaps surprised, but not frustrated, when Henry Fonda played the villain in Sergio Leone's *Once upon a Time in the West.* In the following I call the comic hero played by Woody Allen the Woody persona—to distinguish him from the real human being (who managed to become quite successful by representing the failures of the Woody persona).[2]

Second, Allen is not only a great comedian, he is, being also a good author, even more an excellent screenwriter and movie director. He acquired his capacities as a director slowly, since he began his career as a gag writer and later worked as a stand-up comedian, mainly with words and facial expressions; but, having been interested in films from his childhood on, he was able, in due time, first, to overcome in most of his later screenplays the episodic nature of his early works and achieve that unity and wholeness that is an indispensable prerequisite of great artworks, and, second, to integrate the visual and musical aspects that a good film needs into the stories he conceived. Allen became so good as a director that he needed less of himself as an actor—something that none of the other great film comedians, such as Charlie Chaplin, Buster Keaton, or the Marx Brothers, could have afforded (Chaplin's *A Woman of Paris,* where Chaplin plays only a minor role, was a failure). Not only in those movies that are not at all comic, such as *Interiors* and *September* (which one can regard as Allen's most ambitious and most problematic works, serving mainly to persuade Allen himself that his repertoire as a director was not limited by his innate capacities as an actor), but even in two of his best films, *The Purple Rose of Cairo* and *Bullets over Broadway,*[3] Allen the actor is absent (even if the role of David Shayne probably could have been played by him, were it not for the issue of age); in others, such as *Hannah and Her Sisters,* he no longer plays the central role. There is little doubt that the movies directed by Allen (who is usually, but not always, the only one responsible for the screenplay) and in which he does not act are better and more complex than those in which he only plays and does not serve as director (with the exception of *Play It Again, Sam,* whose screenplay, however, originated with Allen and was based on a play he wrote for the theater). The artistic autonomy the director Allen gained relatively early on vis-à-vis his producers (e.g., regarding the final cut) is, particularly in the United States, uncommon and impressive,[4] and even if the success of his movies also obviously depends on the actors he selects (his reputation allowing him to hire even the most famous stars for compensations they would otherwise not accept), his excellent cinematographers (later ones being Gordon Willis, Carlo Di Palma, Sven Nykvist, and Zhao Fei), the production designer Santo Loquasto, the costume designer Jeffrey Kurland, the editors Susan E. Morse and Alisa Lepselter, and the carefully chosen, evocative music, in the specific case of Woody Allen's films "auteurism"—that is, the approach that regards the director's artistic conception as the center around which film criticism has to gravitate— is widely justified.[5] And in this conception philosophical concerns play a major role. Philosophical issues are important in Allen's movies on two different levels: there are frequent allusions to philosophical problems in the puns and jokes (in the most pronounced form in *Love and Death*), and some of his stories focus in their structure on classical philosophical issues, such as the identity problem in *Play It Again, Sam* and *Zelig,* the shortcomings of the positivist concept of reality in *A Midsummer Night's Sex Comedy,* the relation between reality and art in *The Purple Rose of Cairo* and *Deconstructing Harry,* the objective validity of morality in *Crimes and Misdemeanors* and *Match Point,* the power of evil in *Shadows and Fog,* and the relation between art and morality in *Bullets over Broadway.* It goes without saying that the problems of death and love are omnipresent in Allen's films. One can safely claim that no other living film director addresses the great philosophical issues as openly as Woody Allen does (certainly at the price of his ignoring other important issues, such as social ones, and being quite repetitive), and one can even state that Allen's philosophical vision corresponds exactly to a certain moment in the history of philosophy, namely that moment in the late twentieth century when French existentialism's concept of freedom and its ethically motivated atheism had become profoundly problematic because they seemed to undermine any belief in an objective ethics. If the process of modernity has been also a process of disenchantment of the world, our century at its end came to deep disenchantment with regard to the intrinsic validity and the consequences of a disenchanted moral world for humankind. Atheism might still be regarded by many as true, but the triumphant and optimistic tone in which its message had spread from the late nineteenth century onward gave way to a more somber, if not tormented mode. Allen's films capture this mode without, however, being willing or able to offer a positive solution.[6]

We have approached the third reason why Woody Allen's comedies are philosophically interesting: they have a peculiar position in the history of art. They differ radically from the type of comedy that has been not the only but clearly the dominant strain in the Western tradition since the demise of the Old Comedy and the rise of the Middle and particularly the New Comedy in Greece. I name only one feature: many of his films are not at all realistic. Allen's imaginativeness in developing formal innovations, his vir-tuosity in reinterpreting and parodying older forms of expression (as in his revival of the chorus in *Mighty Aphrodite*), his integration into the comic universe of giant breasts and anxious sperms, extraterrestrials, ghosts, persons in the film within the film, magicians with exorbitant powers, human beings with the capacity to become like their environment or to provoke their environment to fall in love with them, and passengers on the barge of death remind one of Aristophanes. One can even defend the thesis that Allen recovers a fullness of the comic that had been lost by high art— of course with exceptions such as Rabelais and, in some of his plays, Shakespeare—for more than two millennia. An interesting question belonging to that intersection of the philosophy of history and aesthetics, namely the philosophy of the history of art, is why, at the end of the twentieth century, this form of the comic could be successfully revived.

I have indicated the three questions I shall try to answer—the last one only very briefly—in this essay. Why is Allen as a comic actor so funny? What makes some of his films philosophically so profound? What are the causes of this outburst of *vis comica* in a particular historical and cultural setting? First, however, a discussion of the different theories of laughter is indispensable in an essay that is authored not by a film critic but by a philosopher and that hopes to shed light, through its reflections on Woody Allen, on the phenomenon of the comic in general.

Why Do We Laugh, and Why
Are We Justified in Doing So?

In his *Argument of Laughter,* D. H. Monro classifies theories of laughter in four groups: superiority, incongruity, release from restraint, and ambivalence. His own theory on the inappropriate as the common denominator of laughter claims to be a synthesis, but he is well aware that it is quite close to one of the incongruity theories, namely Schopenhauer's.[7] It is easy to see that the incongruity theory is privileged with regard to the others if we focus on humorous laughter (disregarding the nonhumorous forms of laughter, such as laughter from tickling, which most likely are phylogenetically prior but philosophically less interesting, even if the theory is worth mentioning according to which laughter from tickling protected from unwelcome sexual advances; for laughter destroys sexual excitement). For it is the only one to address a feature in the funny or ridiculous object or situation itself, while the other theories deal with features of the recipient. This implies, first, that the incongruity theory is compatible with the other theories, since they deal with different sides of the issue (Bergson's theory, e.g., combines aspects of the superiority and the incongruity theory); and, second, that only the incongruity theory can be the basis of a normative theory of the comic. It is undeniable that different persons, or even the same persons in different moods, laugh at different things; it may well be that when we laugh we feel—either exclusively or simultaneously—superiority, release from restraint, ambivalent emotions; but if we want to answer the question of whether our laughter is intelligent, our feeling of superiority justified, we must analyze the object of laughter. The point I am making exemplifies the more general one that artwork aesthetics must take priority over production or reception aesthetics—even if all three of them are important—because the properties of the artwork provide the criterion of whether a production or reception is appropriate and not vice versa. It may well be that the public of the unnamed comic played by Johnny Haymer in *Annie Hall* really enjoys his stupid jokes and that he himself chuckles for pleasure at the thought of his own superiority— but the point of both the director Allen and the Woody persona Alvy Singer is that what ought to be laughed at is the comic himself, with his grotesque sense of humor and his unjustified feeling of superiority, and certainly not his jokes. It is this fundamental difference between the normative and the descriptive dimension to which the first modern and also crudest form of the superiority theory, the Hobbesian,[8] does not render justice, although it is quite obvious that one important criterion in evaluating other persons is the object of their laughter: a fundamental disharmony of character becomes manifest when a person laughs at things we do not find funny at all and vice versa. Laughter, being fundamentally a reflex mechanism and very hard to simulate in a convincing way (artificial laughter being easily detected), says quite a bit about the persons we are.

Again, these reflections do not entail that at the origin of humankind laughter was elicited by the perception of incongruities—it is very plausible that laughter was simply an expression of joy, well-being, playfulness. Charles Darwin, who has reflected as few other persons have on the expression of our emotions (though he is unfortunately ignored by Monro), writes: "We may confidently believe that laughter, as a sign of pleasure or enjoyment, was practiced by our progenitors long before they deserved to be called human; for very many kinds of monkeys, when pleased, utter a reiterated sound, clearly analogous to our laughter."[9] Darwin recognizes, however, that in humans laughter has a more complex cause: "Something incongruous or unaccountable, exciting surprise and some sense of superiority in the laugher, who must be in a happy frame of mind, seems to be the commonest cause. The circumstances must not be of a momentous nature: no poor man would laugh or smile on suddenly hearing that a large fortune had been bequeathed to him."[10] It is plausible to assume that mediating between laughter caused by the mere feeling of well-being and humorous laughter is that form of laughter triggered by a feeling of superiority. Not only is it not surprising that, in an organism that has to compare itself continuously with other members of the same species, the realization of its own superiority, contrasted with a mishap or a fault of another, may cause a particularly strong feeling of pleasure; the existence of this peculiar form of laughter can be accounted for also by the fact that it may be developed in such a way as to have a positive social function. Indeed, laughter is a painful negative sanction of socially unacceptable behavior (such as vanity), even if it lacks the brutality of physical violence and the risks connected to it. It is therefore a powerful tool to show disapproval without high costs for the user, and this probably explains its evolutionary success—particularly in groups that had to compensate for their inferior power by the strength of their wit, such as the Jews. If the humorous remarks are not directed immediately against the person to be criticized but make a detour, possibly to oneself, and leave the concrete application to the recipients, laughter can even avoid being offensive, and jesters could thus play an important role in political systems in which open criticism of the rulers was not allowed. It is, by the way, too one-sided an interpretation if, along with Mikhail Bakhtin's admirers, one sees in laughter mainly the power to challenge established authorities. Without doubt laughter can fulfill this function, and therefore it is again and again, as, for example, in Rabelais, a means of social change: the inversion of social roles in carnival and the opposition of eating, drinking, and sexual activities, which are in themselves joyful, to loftier ideals are simple and powerful forms of ideology criticism.[11] But laughter's function of criticism or intimidation can also be turned against those who try to change society: Aristophanes was politically a conservative, as were many other satirical and humorous writers. Henri Bergson's essay on laughter develops a more general theory on the social function of laughter: "Laughter is, first, of all, a correction. Created in order to humiliate, it must make a painful impression on the person who is its object. Through it, society revenges itself on the liberties that had been taken with it."[12] Of course, a social subgroup can also laugh at those aspects of the established society that threaten its proper function, but it is plausible to assume that originally it was society at large that defended itself against persons with behavior it regarded as inferior—the larger the audience in a theater, the greater its willingness to laugh.[13] This also explains why, in the traditional theory of genres, only people of the lower classes were regarded as the proper subjects of comedy. One must, however, concede that the public usually was invited to identify with the persons belonging to the lowest class, namely the slaves and later the servants, and with their success in manipulating the vices and stupidity of their aging masters, often to render possible a marriage of the younger generation that the parents wanted to prevent—interclass conflict being combined with intergenerational strife.

With the development of a finer moral sense and a finer intellect, laughter must have become problematic. Sometime in human history it must have begun to be regarded as vulgar to laugh at, for example, a poorer or uglier person (as it occurs in the development of most individuals, who are taught to check their *schadenfreude* and the often cruel or dirty forms of laughter they engaged in as children). The malice, as Bergson rightly notices, inherent in laughter[14] is subjected to moral and aesthetic criticism. This can happen in two ways. On the one hand, there is the merely negative approach, to be found in those moralists who lack any sense of humor and who would like to have laughter banned entirely.[15] On the other hand, there is a wiser, more constructive way to tame that malice, one that still allows for the satisfaction of the ineradicable and fundamentally reasonable human impulse to laugh: namely the cultivation of the sense of the comic by those comic actors and writers who are subtler than others and who resent the vulgarity of their colleagues who have achieved easy successes, for example, by simply mimicking hunchbacked or obese persons. One has only to read the *parabaseis* of some of Aristophanes' comedies or the prologue to Ben Jonson's *Volpone* to see how disgust at cheap humor is an essential characteristic of the great comedians. To those we owe much more than one usually thinks, namely the humanization of our feelings.

To consider laughter morally acceptable, a civilized human being will ask that two conditions be fulfilled. First, the feeling of superiority, which cannot be explained away in the analysis of laughter, will have to be mitigated somehow.

The intelligent laugher has to recognize that the subject he laughs at is not fundamentally different from himself. He may himself share the traits caricatured, but even if this is not directly the case he will know that they are human traits and that he as a human being could well develop them or at least analogous ones, or that he might have been afflicted with them.[16] In cultivated laughter there is, in whatever degree, a certain melancholic identification with the object of laughter—where that is completely lacking, the laugher becomes repulsive or even an object of scorn himself. Perhaps this is the reason why in humans there is a certain continuum between smiles and laughter,[17] although in our apelike ancestors they must have had almost opposed functions—with laughter expressing a feeling of happiness and superiority, smiling a feeling of submission, often to ward off an attack. This latter function of smiles is well known also in humans,[18] and it is the more surprising that nevertheless a smile can sometimes announce laughter, that an expression belonging to the behavior of appeasement may prepare the expression of a behavior originally linked to the enjoyment of one's own superiority. Perhaps the reason behind it is the following: the laugher who first smiles asks in a certain sense for forgiveness for what he is going to do, partly to avoid retaliation on another occasion, but partly, perhaps, also because even if such retaliation is not to be feared he has an unconscious insight into his affinity with the comic object. This explains why often, although not always, the peculiar emotional quality of laughter is an ambivalent feeling, sometimes of simultaneous attraction and repulsion with regard to its object (where this is a person), who is pitied (i.e., identified with) and scorned (i.e., distanced) at the same time.

The degree of identification with the object of laughter depends on various factors. One is the inner consistency of the ridiculous person. The way Don Quixote reacts to Sancho Panza's objections against his interpretations of reality causes more laughter not only because it shows the extent of his madness but also because it elicits a certain admiration with regard to his capacity to make sense of his theory—a capacity in itself positive, without which also scientific creativity would be impossible. Another factor is whether the ridiculous person succeeds in making us laugh at an even more ridiculous one, as is usually the case with the parasites in ancient comedies, such as Gnatho in Terence's *Eunuch,* who is morally reprehensible but clearly superior to his master, Thraso. The decisive quality is, however, the comic person's capacity to laugh at herself: because in doing so she joins the spectators or readers, they, having this trait in common, are much more prone to identify with her and thus laugh with her, not at her. Probably the important difference between the satiric and the comic mood, which are both related to laughter,[19] has to do with this capacity— Jonson's *Volpone* being a satiric and Aristophanes' *Peace* a comic example: one laughs at Volpone (and even more at his victims, who are not less greedy but more stupid), but one laughs with Trygaios. The figure of Falstaff in Shakespeare's *Henry IV* and *The Merry Wives of Windsor* and, even more, in Boito's libretto for Verdi's opera (one of the few librettos that can claim to be a great artwork) shows that a transition exists between the two moods: we laugh sometimes at, sometimes with Falstaff, the latter particularly when he joins the persons laughing at him. In this aspect the Woody persona is, as we will see, closely related to Falstaff. Because of his increased self-awareness, the comic hero is more individualized than the subject of a satire: satiric comedies may have titles indicating an abstract quality (as in Molière's *The Miser*), or the names of the persons may be animal names (as in *Volpone,* where a Doctor Lupus is mentioned, the same name given to the beauty surgeon in *Celebrity*), but if we want to laugh with a person individualization is indispensable.

Not only the emotional quality of laughter but also its objects have to be of a certain nature if laughter is to be acceptable. The persons laughed at must deserve our scorn because their mishap is a just consequence of their behavior and their behavior contradicts some intellectual or moral norm one cannot help acknowledging. This contradiction between a certain behavior and the relevant norm explains why only some form of incongruity theory can claim to capture the reason why an intelligent person is allowed or even invited to laugh at a given piece of behavior. We are justified in laughing when we are right in feeling superior, and we are right in feeling superior when the derided behavior is indeed something that ought to be avoided and when by laughing we acknowledge certain standards also for ourselves and oblige ourselves not to infringe on certain rules—if we should do so, we know that we, too, will be ridiculed. However, the main problem of the incongruity theory is the precise determination of the class of incongruities that make us laugh, and I must immediately concede that I neither know of a theory giving the necessary and the sufficient conditions of that class nor have one to offer myself. I will thus limit myself to discussing the plausibility and the limits both of the first modern and of the relatively richest theories of incongruity, namely those of Schopenhauer and Bergson.

The first important incongruity theory stems, as already mentioned, from Schopenhauer, who expands in a fascinating way Kant's enigmatic allusions. Laughter, according to Schopenhauer, originates from the sudden perception of an incongruity between a concept and the objects we perceive by way of that concept. The incongruity can occur by beginning either with concrete objects, which are unified under an encompassing concept, or with the concept, under which very different objects are subsumed. The first case constitutes witticism *(Witz),* the second foolishness *(Narrheit).*[20] Witticism is always intentional—we laugh with the joke teller at someone or something else, not at him—and it is conceptual or verbal. Puns can be subsumed under it, though here it is no longer different objects unified under the same concept but different concepts unified under the same word. Foolishness causes laughter in an unintentional way and manifests itself mostly in actions; it encompasses pedanticism, the desire to subject reality to abstract concepts. The art of the jester consists in masking his witticism as foolishness: we laugh at him even if his intent, like that of the witty joke teller, is to make us laugh. While irony is fun hidden behind seriousness, humor is seriousness hidden behind fun.[21] Schopenhauer develops his theory in the context of his empiricist epistemology, which insists on the priority of perceptions over concepts. For him, laughter is the revenge we take against reason when we see that its concepts do not really fit the subtle differences of reality.[22] The immediate advantage of Schopenhauer's formula is that it takes into account epistemological inadequacies and puns, which are neglected by other theories. But his siding with perception overlooks that the failure may be on both sides—when Hippias answers the Socratic question of what beauty is with "a beautiful girl,"[23] it is he who is made fun of, not the generality of concepts. In some of the jokes Schopenhauer offers yet fails to analyze properly, the humorous effect is based on their self-reference, particularly on the contradiction between what is said and what is done. Also a simple contradiction between two concepts, and not concepts and objects, can sometimes be funny. It is furthermore certainly possible to expand Schopenhauer's theory by insisting that the general concept often traces connections between two realms that evoke very different emotional responses, thereby contributing to a reversal of values that not only may be funny but may hint at a profound truth. "Our mental exploration may uncover a real connection between our mental compartments." Monro continues this remark by stating that the addition of other elements such as codes of values, satirical intent, and emotional attitudes transcends what Schopenhauer is explicitly stating even if it is compatible with it.[24] Indeed, an assimilation toward the worse or toward the better, to name the concepts used in the most important ancient treatise on comedy,[25] even if it is not necessary, certainly increases the humorous effect. To give two examples, in *Scoop* Sid Waterman explains, "I was born in the Hebrew persuasion, but I converted to narcissism." The concept of conversion entails the transformation of a person by his opening himself to a higher dimension; narcissism, however, is the opposite of transcending one's self, even if it is true that it has features of a religion, for it renders the self absolute and has become a widespread ideology. In *Manhattan* Ike says to his seventeen-year-old girlfriend Tracy: "I don't believe in extramarital relationships. I think people should mate for life, like pigeons or Catholics."[26] This remark is witty in a Schopenhauerian way because it brings two very different things, pigeons and Catholics, under one general concept, monogamous behavior. But it is easy to see that other factors add to its comic effect. By introducing "pigeons" between "people" and "Catholics," the remark surreptitiously diminishes the value of the behavior praised; for one can hardly regard animals as models, and to compare pigeons with Catholics is clearly disparaging to the latter. So there is an implicit criticism of the monogamous ideal that Ike nevertheless tries to defend and Tracy questions. But not only is there a contradiction between different parts of the statement (the criticism of extramarital relationships and the praise of pigeons); there is also a contradiction between the statement and its speaker. Ike has gone through two divorces, and his remarks are triggered by the encounter with Mary, the mistress of his married friend Yale. Even before the later development of the story, his behavior during this encounter betrays the main reason for his disapproval of Yale's relationship—namely that he himself is getting interested in Mary and wants to get rid of Tracy, who, despite her doubts about monogamy, exhibits till the end a touching fidelity. One can therefore say that Ike is the reverse of Schopenhauer's jester—Ike's intentional witticism, which playfully undermines what he says, is foolish because it reveals to the intelligent spectator of the film (although not to Tracy, who is too much in love and too candid for that) the real desires that he himself is not yet prepared to acknowledge.

Another addition to Schopenhauer's theory is possible, and it is particularly fruitful with regard to film theory—there may be in a film a contrast between images, words, and music. Virgil's line in *Take the Money and Run* regarding his first walk with Louise, whom he originally wanted to rob—"Within fifteen minutes I wanted to marry her . . . after half an hour, I gave up all thoughts of stealing her purse"—is funny in itself, for one would think that the first intent entailed the second immediately, not after fifteen minutes. But the contrast is heightened by the romantic, almost kitschy images of the couple wandering about together. Allen has devised various techniques to increase our perception of comic contrasts; thus in *Annie Hall* the splitting of the screen contrasts the mutual expectations or interpretations that different persons have of the same situation, and the appearance on the screen of subtitles reveals the thoughts persons have while speaking. The juxtaposition of Alvy's remark to Annie that "photography's interesting, 'cause, you know, it's—it's a new art form, and a, uh, a set of aesthetic criteria have not emerged yet" and his thought "I wonder what she looks like naked?" is comic not only because of the contrast between the intellectual discussion and the more worldly afterthoughts but also because there is a Schopenhauerian close connection between the lofty concept of aesthetics and the basic experience of the beauty of a naked body. In its crudest form the contrast between image and words is the point of Allen's remake of *Kagi no Kagi* as *What's Up, Tiger Lily?,* in which he kept the images but radically changed the words.

It is Bergson's merit to have somehow generalized Schopenhauer's theory. The breadth and depth of his analysis of the comic features of forms, movements, situations, words, and characters, the splendor of his style, and the skillful combination of the superiority and incongruity theories into a unity make his book extremely persuasive. For Bergson laughter is society's sanction against those who try to impose something mechanical on the flux of life. Fundamentally the perceived (not necessarily the real) rigidity of movements and characters makes them comic because they contradict one of the main demands of life, elasticity. The comic is therefore opposed not so much to beauty as to grace. Grimaces, mechanical movements, masquerading, the overwhelming of the mind by the body, the reification of persons, repetition, inversion, the interference of different series (being opposed to the organic traits of continuous change, irreversibility, and an individuality closed in itself), the insertion of an absurdity into a sacred formula, the literal understanding of metaphors, transposition into a different tone (degradation and exaggeration), unsociability, obstinacy, distraction, automatisms of character—all these phenomena, most of which play an important role in Allen, are paraded in review by Bergson and connected by the common idea that they all violate the essence of life. One certainly has to agree with Bergson that many cases can be subsumed under this idea. The reason why we laugh at the mechanical steps of Prussian soldiers, their *Stechschritt,* is that they are in contrast with normal and healthy movement: it is not reasonable to refuse to bend the knees, since they are integral for walking. The overwhelming comic power of Charlie Chaplin's *Modern Times,* to name the most Bergsonian of all comedies—and of its imitations at the beginning of *Bananas* when Fielding tests the "Execusizor" or in many scenes in *Sleeper,* such as when Miles simulates being a robot (with movements reminiscent of Fernand Leger's *Mechanical Ballet*) or Luna enters the "Orgasmotron"—stems from the subjection of a living human being to the mechanisms of engines and industrial society in general, from the reification of a person.

But is this always the case? Think of repetition, which Bergson rightly regards as a fundamental strategy of the comic and which Allen uses as early as *Casino Royale* when Jimmy Bond manages to escape execution by a firing squad by jumping over the wall, only to find on the other side another firing squad at work. Is not repetition a basic feature of life? Do not organisms have to face violent death over and over? And does not our laughter protest against the repetition of the same accident or the same silly behavior by the same person because human dignity or morality—though certainly not life—demands a person's continuous development and progress? Is not one of the most important points of *Midsummer Night's Sex Comedy* (which distinguishes it from Ingmar Bergman's related work *Smiles of a Summer Night*) that repetitions of earlier situations cannot work because the knowledge that it is a repetition irrevocably distinguishes the new situation from the earlier analogous one—knowledge being a spiritual, not a vital category? Think of inversion, a no less basic comic structure. When in Ernst Lubitsch's *To Be or Not to Be* Josef Tura first plays Col. Ehrhardt vis-à-vis the real Professor Siletsky and then is brought as the false Siletsky to the real Col. Ehrhardt, we laugh with Tura because he has been able to anticipate, at least to a certain degree, the real Ehrhardt, and we laugh at Ehrhardt because it has been so easy to predict his behavior. But anticipation of another person's behavior is a deed of spirit, not of mere life. Even where the comic force of inversion is of a different kind, it does not rest on recognition of the superiority of life to nonlife. When in Allen's best short story, "The Kugelmass Episode," which in 1977 won the O. Henry Award as best short story of the year, the magician, unable to solve the personal problems he has caused Kugelmass by bringing Madame Bovary to New York, says, "I'm a magician, not an analyst," we laugh because we remember the desperate remark of the analyst who could not help Kugelmass: "After all, I'm an analyst, not a magician."[27] We laugh because we see a form of retribution[28] at work, as when, in *A Midsummer Night's Sex Comedy,* Leopold and Maxwell meet unexpectedly before dinner with analogous, even if subtly different intentions, or when, in *Radio Days,* Uncle Abe goes to the atheistic Waldbaums to remind them of their Jewish heritage and returns as a convinced communist; and it pleases us to find out that even powerful magicians can be as helpless as analysts, who never would have thought that even magicians could need their cooperation, that someone interested in another person's partner might suffer the same fate as the other person, that the converter might be converted himself. But this rehabilitation appeals to our sense of justice, not to our admiration for the categories of life. Consider the interference of different series: when Danny Rose through a misunderstanding gets pursued by the Mafia, we laugh because of the contrasts, first, between this kind man and the mob and, second, between his clumsiness and the idea that he is a seducer, but hardly because interference is rare among the haphazards of life. Think of vulgarity: does not its concept convey the idea that also an utterly healthy behavior may be inappropriate, and inappropriate because it contradicts the norms of spirituality, not those of life? Walter Holander, the caterer of Allen's first (and mediocre) play *Don't Drink the Water,* is funny because he is vulgar, and he is vulgar because he is not spiritual—he certainly does not violate the norms of average vitality.

A reflection may be added on one of the greatest comic figures of all time, Don Quixote, whom Bergson names only a few times (probably because *Don Quixote* is not a product of French literature, from which the great majority of Bergson's examples are drawn). Of course Don Quixote is comic partly because of his incapacity to accept the norms of his society and to enjoy life in a normal, vital manner. But his incapacity is also a refusal, and with the development of the novel this refusal gains an increasing sublimity that, paradoxically, is recognized also by the person who, through the effect of contrast, increases the comic aspects of Don Quixote, namely Sancho Panza. One may be comic by underachieving the norms of life, but if this underachievement betrays that one was aiming at something higher than life, the comic and the sublime cross, and a new dimension of ambivalence is added to our laughter. We laugh at the person who is unable to adapt to the norms of life and society, but we laugh at his failure also because it represents a challenge to these norms. Alceste in Molière's *The Misanthrope* is, as Bergson rightly points out, funny because of his rigidity, but in our cordial laughter at him there is mixed a satiric laughter at the society around him that obliges him to withdraw from it.[29] It is this dimension that Bergson misses. One cannot help feeling that an exhaustive theory of humorous laughter would need a more general idea of inadequacy and that inadequacy with regard to the norms of organic life is only one, albeit very important, example. Bergson is misled by his vitalism to regard life as the ultimate criterion of normativity, but there is no reason to do so, as there is no reason to mistrust the capacity of concepts to grasp reality. Of course, concepts and theories fail again and again in the face of reality, but the alternative is not a metaphysical opposition of reality and concepts, only the elaboration of better concepts.

All codes of values involve a certain rigidity, just because they are codes. To discard one code in favor of another, then, is not to escape from rigidity. When humour reverses values, it may well be that it exposes some ready-made generalization as inapplicable in a given case; but there will always be some other generalization lurking in the background. We have seen that humour is sometimes aimed at the eccentric who will not conform to a code, and sometimes at the code itself. In either case the appeal is to some code of values; either the standard which the code represents, or another which transcends it. Probably it is because Bergson realizes this that he is prepared to convict the eccentric of rigidity, but not the code. For ultimately humour appeals to a code of values even when it escapes from one.[30]

But if the incongruity of reason with regard to empirical objects and the incongruity of rigidity with regard to life are not the only forms of incongruity that cause laughter, if other forms may be humorous as well, why does not every incongruity or inappropriateness make us laugh? Clearly there are restricting conditions outside which even the most blatant inappropriateness will not be experienced as funny. For an incongruity to cause laughter, we must, first, be in some joyous mood. Even the best jokes won't make a person laugh who is in utter despair because he has just lost a beloved one, or is thinking intensely of something else, or has a merely theoretical interest in analyzing the structure of the comic. On the other hand, once a comedian has succeeded in making us begin to laugh, he needs less and less effort to maintain us in this state. If his facial expression is comic, if it creates a comic spirit, we will laugh even if his jokes are mediocre—jokes that, if told by another, would make us yawn.

Second, even if the person going to a comedy expects to laugh, a moment of surprise with regard to the content is important.[31] The pleasure inherent in such laughter is probably linked to that felt when we make an unexpected discovery that seems to confirm our high opinion of ourselves. We usually no longer laugh at a joke we have heard several times—if we laugh, we laugh at the person who seems to have forgotten that he already entertained us with his joke or play with the situation of its repetition. Just this reflection shows us, however, that surprise is not indispensable: we may laugh at the repetition of someone's compulsive behavior, particularly if we have been able to anticipate it. The "Uff" of Hilmar Tønnesen in Ibsen's *Pillars of Society* shows the intellectual horizon of that character. An extremely comic repetition in an Allen movie that highlights a character trait is the following: Nancy in *Bananas* has broken off with Fielding Mellish because "something is missing," thereby driving him to San Marcos, where he becomes that country's leader. In a state visit to the United States, he once again meets Nancy, who does not recognize him but falls in love with him as the admired political leader of San Marcos. After a wonderful night together—for Nancy "practically a religious experience"—he informs her of his true identity, and not only is she not overwhelmed by the changes Fielding has undergone to prove worthy of her, but she shouts disappointedly that she knew something was missing—and we know that this woman cannot be helped. Obviously in such cases our feeling of superiority is elicited, but one must add that the ultimate reason why such repetitions (which must not have been intended by the object of laughter) are so comic is that they contradict our normative expectations that a person will undergo development and progress (not, as we have seen, the norms of life). A slightly different but related case occurs when the repetition of the same words in contrasting situations is felt as comic not because it shows a person's bizarre passion but, on the contrary, because it betrays the emptiness of the words with regard to the person's real being: a good example is Ken Post's identical apologies in very different situations in *Another Woman.*

Third, the incongruity that makes us laugh cannot be too brutal—this is Aristotle's point that the object of laughter is what is ugly but neither painful nor injurious.[32] There are many comedies about misers and lechers, but hardly any on successful murderers—for we must not feel threatened by the object of our laughter.[33] Bergson is right when he remarks that even Tartuffe is comic only as long as we assume that his hypocrisy has become his second nature—if, on the contrary, we see in him mainly a mastermind we will detest him but not be amused.[34] Lester in *Crimes and Misdemeanors* is certainly not profound, but his comments on tragedy and comedy converge with Aristotle's: "If it bends, it's funny, if it breaks, it's not funny." The murder of Dolores can never become funny, at least as long as we see her as a real human being; and her pains as well as her faults are described far too realistically to make it possible not to see her in this light. The legitimate human desire to feel superior even in the face of death explains, though, why black humor could and had to develop, as the remarkable attempt to overcome the fear of death constituting the *conditio humana.* One has to notice, however, that black humor usually focuses on cartoonlike figures or on persons of the past with whom a concrete identification is no longer possible (in this sense Lester's dictum that comedy is tragedy plus time is not completely off the mark, even if in its context it betrays Lester's superficiality). In the case of a person presently to die, only this person herself, not a bystander, could make a joke belonging to the genre of black humor without violating the decorum and destroying the sympathy the situation evokes, which is not compatible with the distancing inherent in laughter. (Grand examples of comic behavior in the face of death are Mercutio's last puns in *Romeo and Juliet* and the parody of Prussian *Stechschritt* in Roberto Benigni's *La vita è bella* that the father, who is about to be shot shortly before the liberation of the mass extermination camp, performs to diffuse the fear of, and thereby save the life of, his child.) Another situation in which black humor may be a legitimate form of the comic is when the framework is clearly not realistic.[35] In comic dramas or films like F. Dürrenmatt's *The Physicists* or Stanley Kubrick's *Dr. Strangelove,* the death of the nurses or the soldiers is indeed negligible, since the world proves to be in the hands of madmen. One finds a nonrealistic setting in *Bananas,* in *Love and Death,* and, to a lesser degree, because mixed with the suggestion of real horror, also in *Shadows and Fog,* Allen's films with the greatest numbers of deaths: when during the revolution in *Bananas* we see a tumbling carriage reminding us of Eisenstein's *Battleship Potemkin,* we know it is more a movie about our clichés on revolution than about revolution itself. In *Manhattan Murder Mystery* the tension between the comic atmosphere and the murder is lessened by the inclusion of films in the film, an inclusion that has an impact on the action but at the same time diminishes the credibility of the "real" killings within the film. In *Bullets over Broadway* the godfather, Nick Valenti, is presented so unrealistically that we do not take seriously the murders that he orders (furthermore, the last and decisive one happens on stage and is regarded by the public within the film as part of the plot), let alone his girlfriend Olive's grotesque voice, which strongly contributes to the surrealistic atmosphere of the film and which everybody is happy to have silenced. All these deaths are far less emotionally affecting than Eve's suicide in *Interiors* or the murder of Nola Rice and her neighbor Mrs. Eastby in *Match Point,* Allen's most tragic works to date, while the latter's predecessor *Crimes and Misdemeanors* combines a tragic and a comic strand in an unusual way. (Novels, tragedies, and comedies in which two parallel actions take place are well known, to name only two authors, from Tolstoy and Shakespeare, but the mixture of radically different emotional moods is rare.) One can therefore hardly reproach Allen for writing comedies on subjects that deserve a tragic treatment; but the opposite criticism may perhaps apply to *September,* where problems are taken seriously that do not merit it—or at least do not merit a melodramatic treatment, but only the half-melancholy, half-ironic treatment of Chekhov, whom Allen vainly attempts to emulate. The structure that A loves B, B C, and C D is fundamentally a comic one, as Shakespeare, Bergman, and Allen prove in their midsummer night's plays, and its solution can only be to form happy couples, not to produce universal sadness and bitterness.

When in *Love and Death* a man tries to sell blintzes to the soldiers engaged in the battle, we laugh because we know that the persons we see are not really dying. We enjoy the scene because it subtly subverts the code of military values. But if we are sincere we cannot deny the possibility that a small part of our pleasure in farcical cruelty may originate from its satisfaction of our aggressive impulses. The hypothesis I am considering is, of course, known from Freud's *Jokes and Their Relation to the Unconscious.* In this extremely rich book, Freud, after having investigated in detail the techniques of jokes, addresses the question of their purpose. He distinguishes between innocent and tendentious jokes, the latter satisfying sexual, aggressive, blasphemous, or skeptical needs. His theory that the pleasure of innocent jokes results from economy in psychic expenditure remains debatable (the related one that relief from the compulsion of rationality is at the root of the pleasure of jokes is more plausible and reminiscent of Schopenhauer); but his analysis of tendentious jokes is utterly convincing. We are usually inhibited from satisfying our sexual or aggressive desires; but if there is the possibility of doing so through an allusion in a joke, circumvention of the inner censor becomes possible.

> The repressive activity of civilization brings it about that primary possibilities of enjoyment, which have now, however, been repudiated by the censorship in us, are lost to us. But to the human psyche all renunciation is exceedingly difficult, and so we find that tendentious jokes provide a means of undoing the renunciation and retrieving what was lost. When we laugh at a refined obscene joke, we are laughing at the same thing that makes a peasant laugh at a coarse piece of smut. In both cases the pleasure springs from the same source. We, however, could never bring ourselves to laugh at the coarse smut; we should feel ashamed or it would seem to us disgusting. We can only laugh when a joke has come to our help.[36]

Children, as we have seen before, laugh at many things that they are taught to ignore as they become adults—scatological objects probably more often than sexual ones, but also physical deformities of other human beings. It would be mean if a comedian made us laugh at obesity as such. But the temptation to laugh at it can be satisfied with good conscience if the comedian links it to something that contrasts with it; then the contrast elicits the intellectual pleasure that allows us to laugh, even if an honest analysis will find that this pleasure is heightened by the simultaneous satisfaction of the primordial and repressed desire to ridicule obesity. Allen uses this strategy at least twice: in *Stardust Memories* Irene, small and fat, with a blond ponytail and a bruised face, certainly not a beautiful woman, wears a garment on which is written in fancy letters "Sexy"; in the similar *Celebrity* a teenage obese acrobat makes a short appearance. Legitimate laughter is triggered in both cases by the sharp contrast between obesity, on the one hand, and sexual attractiveness and acrobatic talent respectively, on the other; and the whole structure of the film makes it clear that the main object of scorn is not so much single individuals as a society that compels persons to declare themselves sexy and grants the status of rising celebrities to persons like skinheads, overweight achievers, hookers, Mafia godfathers, and teenage obese acrobats, who, as in Federico Fellini's *Ginger & Fred,* are invited to TV shows. But this complex comic structure rests on the childish laughter at obesity—much as the complicated form of human sexuality that the Woody persona incorporates presupposes the inexhaustible *vis comica* of sexual jokes.

Being Funny by Being Witty:
The Essence of the Woody Persona

The essence of the Woody persona remains astonishingly constant through all the movies: Sandy Bates is more successful than Alvy Singer, but his personality is quite similar (he could be Singer fifteen years later); the jester Felix lives in the Middle Ages, Boris Grushenko lives in the early nineteenth century, Hobbes, Zelig, Kleinman, and CW Briggs live in the first half of the twentieth century, and Miles Monroe wakes up in 2174, but their psychology does not differ much from that of the majority of the avatars of the Woody persona who live in our time. Only with regard to the heroes living in the first half of the twentieth century is there an effort to represent the cultural setting of that period; Felix and Boris enjoy the anachronisms they continuously commit. Most of the contemporary instantiations of the Woody persona live in New York, even if this is not an essential trait. But it is so peculiar a trait that Alvy Singer in *Annie Hall,* with three Oscars and a fourth nomination Allen's most awarded film, can claim to be particularly close to the Woody persona, while we smile at Nick Fifer in *Scenes from a Mall,* a film directed by Paul Mazursky, for living in Los Angeles, and we laugh when he tells his wife that he does not want to have a dinner guest praise New York's intellectual life over L.A.—something Alvy Singer would love to do. In any case, the Woody persona is utterly urban, like most of Allen's heroes—Robin Simon in *Celebrity,* exhorted by a priest to open up to the wonders of nature around her, asks whether there are ticks; she does not want to get Lyme disease. Even Boris Grushenko, who grows up in the countryside, does not love nature; it is for him mainly "an enormous restaurant," "spiders and bugs and big fish eating little fish and plants eating plants." Renata in *Interiors* has, after looking at trees, a vision that frightens her—"everything seems . . . sort of awful . . . and predatory."[37] And in the film that is the director Allen's most beautiful tribute to nature, *A Midsummer Night's Sex Comedy,* the Woody persona, Andrew Hobbes, is not at all at home in nature. Note that in Boris's case the mistrust of nature is based on a moral protest against its brutality—a pantheism à la Spinoza will never satisfy the Woody persona or Allen himself as an alternative to theism. Like Schopenhauer, the Woody persona and Allen seem to think that if theism has to be relinquished, atheism is the only intellectually plausible alternative.

What are the factors that render the Woody persona so irresistibly funny? The trait that comes immediately to mind is, obviously, his tormented relation with women and with his own sexuality, so reminiscent of Kafka's heroes. As we shall see, this relation is linked to the peculiar form of failure that characterizes the attempts of the Woody persona, a form of failure, though, that in an odd way can also be considered a success. (Where the failure is complete and the Woody persona only bitter, as in the case of the pathological David Dobel, he quickly becomes uninteresting.) This strange mixture of triumph and defeat also determines his intellectuality: the Woody persona is obviously an intellectual who feels threatened both by overcaring mother figures and by physically stronger men. But neither can he compete with academic intellectuals, toward whom he entertains a spiteful animosity. Despite his antiacademic resentment, his greatest admirers are academics because they recognize that he X-rays their flaws and that he, and not they, ask the really important, existential questions. There is, finally, a profound ambivalence with regard to the problem of whether we laugh at or with the Woody persona. For he is not simply a comic object of laughter—he knows that he is funny and is extremely witty about it, so that he intentionally makes his interlocutors (and the public) laugh. Yet through his witty jokes he is funny again. How is this possible?

Allen, even more than Woody, masters all the techniques of jokes, but it is easy to see that his favorite ones are inflation and its inversion, deflation, the sudden juxtaposition of something trivial after something sublime (whether it is a concept or a high-sounding word: "I am polymorphously perverse," claims the supermodel in *Celebrity,* using an expression from Freud). Although the two techniques are obviously different, they have a similar effect, for by praising something banal in high terms one implicitly also devalues the sphere to which these terms belong. Good examples of inflation, related to the act of eating, so important in Allen, are "Fabrizio's: Criticism and Response," where the language of literary critics is hilariously applied to the review of a restaurant, and the biography of the fictitious inventor of the sandwich, the Earl of Sandwich, in "Yes, but Can the Steam Engine Do This?"[38] The very old subgenres of comedy, parody and travesty, are based on inflation—comic heroes imitate, intentionally or not, tragic heroes and their language, and even if the main effect is to ridicule the latter, the comic hero sometimes partakes of the splendor of the tragic one. Allen, whose knowledge of film history inspires awe, is a master of parody and travesty.[39] Sometimes he simply transposes certain "lower" film genres in a different mood—documentaries in *Take the Money and Run,* historical costume films with a Shakespearean flavor and horror movies (along with TV quiz shows) in *Everything* (which is itself a parody of a self-help sex book by a Dr. David Reuben, who, of course, did not like the film), science fiction movies in *Sleeper*—with the clear intent to make fun of them. But by quoting Ingmar Bergman's *The Seventh Seal* in *Love and Death* he bestows on his own film a peculiar poetic quality and exhorts us to look for a deeper meaning behind the funny episodes.

Deflation is exemplified best by the aphorisms at the end of "My Philosophy," "Eternal nothingness is O.K. if you are dressed for it" and "Not only is there no God, but try getting a plumber on weekends" being the most witty.[40] "Eternal nothingness" seems to be a profound metaphysical concept, but already the colloquial "O.K." deflates it, and the allusion to one's dress explodes it. There is an immediate contradiction between nothingness and every concrete object, but since dressing has to do with personal vanity, which the thought of nothingness should annihilate, the contradiction becomes even more glaring. Note that the joke is directed not so much against the idea of nothingness as against the cultural establishment that discusses it well dressed; it makes fun more of pretentious intellectuals than of the concept. Something analogous is true of the second aphorism. Its first half contains such an important proposition that one asks oneself how anything could be added to it, as the "not only" announces. The second half, however, is so utterly out of proportion with it, as the change of mood already suggests, that the whole sentence becomes almost grotesque. But it would be misleading to believe that the aphorism is intended mainly to ridicule religious belief; it satirizes as well persons for whom the supposed death of God is less devastating than the obstruction of their toilet, and it makes fun of the abyss between profound theories and the banalities of life humans are supposed to deal with every day. It is this ambivalence that makes Allen's jokes so good.

But not only is the director and screenwriter Allen witty, the witty Woody persona is also funny, due partly to the use of his physiognomy, in a way that the writer Allen is not. I shall give five examples that are different enough to show the range of Allen's intermingling of the two qualities. In *Manhattan Murder Mystery* Larry Lipton sits with his wife, Carol, at a Wagner opera, obviously on her suggestion. He is bored and insists on leaving in the middle, with the argument that he does not want to get an urge to conquer Poland. The remark is witty in its combining of two heterogeneous spheres, music and the military, and also a very good joke because it is a historical fact that Wagner's music fascinated Hitler and many national socialists, so that a case can indeed be made that it evokes our more brutal instincts. But the remark, as uttered by the Woody persona, is also funny, for it sheds light on the marriage problems of the Liptons and conjures up the absurd image of the asthenic Lipton (who elsewhere confesses that he prefers "atrophy" to exercise) conquering Poland. And some of this fun must be clear not only to Allen but also to the Woody persona, who in all his avatars has a tendency to self-deprecation and knows very well that he is not a physical hero. We laugh with Allen, we laugh at Woody, but we laugh also with Woody. In *Stardust Memories* Sandy Bates speaks with his sister Debby about their elderly mother. Debby mentions that she is now blind in one eye and deaf in one ear. Sandy reacts: "Oh. I hope the same side of the head, right? Because that's important, so she's even" and, exhorted not to make jokes, continues: "She should be, even at that age.... It's very—"[41] Here again the comic operates on different levels. On the one hand,

35

Sandy's remark is a joke belonging to the genre of black humor: it opposes a positive ideal structure, evenness, to two very bad real things. But as we have said above, jokes of this sort in relation to a real person (other than oneself) are tasteless, particularly with regard to one's own mother. Now the funny thing is that Sandy does not at all want to make fun of his mother. Since he is, or perhaps has been, a director of comic movies and has been obliged for two days to smile at everybody and say something personal to all sorts of unattractive fans at a festival dedicated to his films, his joke is a reflex, betraying the *déformation professionelle* of the comedian. Sandy tries to be kind and considerate to a very old person ("even at that age"), and it is just funny that in trying to do so he ends up being the opposite, namely cruel. In *Shadows and Fog*, Max Kleinman, pursued by a mob that wants to lynch him, takes refuge in the house of his former fiancée, Alma. He had failed to appear on the appointed day of their wedding when he was discovered having sex with her sister in a broom closet (this allusion to insatiable sexual appetite, by the way, fits other forms of the Woody persona but is quite at odds with Kleinman's personality). Alma has not forgiven him: not only does she drive him out of her house, knowing full well that this will lower his chances of survival, but she even loads a gun to take her revenge. Kleinman flees with the remark that he is happy she is not bitter about her past. This remark seems to be simply ironic—irony consisting in saying the contrary of what one is thinking, often to test the intelligence of the interlocutor. But irony is grounded in a feeling of superiority, and Kleinman does not look at all as if he feels superior. On the contrary, he is dominated by the desire to please and satisfy the persons he is dealing with, so that it is quite possible that his objectively ironic remark is subjectively an attempt to appease Alma—and this is funny indeed.

Analogously ambivalent is Lee Simon's answer to the publisher who asks him about his book project, namely that it has floated. The answer is extremely funny because the spectator of *Celebrity* (but probably not the publisher, who understands the verb metaphorically) knows that the manuscript was indeed thrown into the water by a woman who took understandable revenge on Lee for his having left her for another woman the day she moved into his apartment. The usual comic strategy is to misunderstand a metaphor literally; here we have the inversion—a verb is understood metaphorically that ought to be interpreted literally. However, the misunderstanding is of a peculiar nature because Lee certainly does not want the publisher to know about the details of his failure as a writer; and it is not even clear whether his remark is a conscious witticism, a Freudian lapse or—most likely—what one could call a frozen witticism, a remark once produced with bitter humor and then carried on by habit. If witticisms have the function of challenging mechanical rigidity imposed on life, frozen witticisms are funny in the extreme. *Annie Hall* begins and ends with jokes that the narrator and comic hero Alvy Singer tells the audience. The jokes, one of which is traced back by Alvy to no lesser a figure than Freud, are excellent. "I would never wanna belong to any club that would have someone like me for a member" (which goes back to Groucho Marx) sums up the fundamental problem of the Woody persona, his self-contempt, masked as arrogance, which renders a reciprocal love relation with another person utterly impossible because he could love only the persons who would reject him, whether they are his lovers or, as in *Stardust*

Memories, his fans. No less witty and somehow related is the joke at the end about the man who tells a doctor that his brother is crazy since he believes he is a chicken but, asked to turn him in, refuses to do so because he needs the eggs; it is easier to see madness in others than in oneself, even if one shares and abets it. But why are the jokes also funny? Because the jokes are, along with his first play, inspired by his own life story but with a happy ending, all that remains to Alvy after the breakup with Annie. To be reduced to telling good jokes is sad, even if one has the intelligence and honesty to know that the jokes apply to oneself. Alvy Singer is as lonely with his jokes as Harry Block with his literary creations, and in both cases it is clear that the intellectuality of the Woody persona is both a cause of and a compensation for his difficulties with normal life. One laughs with Alvy about his jokes, but one laughs also at him—and does the latter along with him. It is this utmost reflexivity that makes the Woody persona so original and fascinating but also so desolate—for reflexivity in this peculiar form ultimately bars access to others and to life.

Not only is the Woody persona witty and funny at the same time, but he is simultaneously intellectual and antiacademic. The combination of these two traits becomes particularly clear in the famous scene of lining up at a movie theater in *Annie Hall.* Annie, who overslept and missed her therapy appointment that morning, is attacked by Alvy for having made a hostile gesture toward him. She counters, asking if he thinks that way because of their sexual probems. Alvy does not like the expression "*our* sexual problems" and provokes a loud and furious reaction from Annie, which causes the man in front of them to turn and to look at them: "Okay, I'm very sorry. *My* sexual problem! Okay, *my* sexual problem! Huh?" Alvy, perplexed by the public interest they are arousing, tries to save the situation: "I never read that. That was—that was Henry James, right? Novel, uh, the sequel to *Turn of the Screw? My Sexual*. . ." The remark is brilliant for different reasons. First, misunderstandings are a popular source of comic effects—if the meaning intended and the meaning understood contrast, they instantiate a comic inadequacy. In this case, however, the misunderstanding is faked—it is witty and not funny, or better: it is funny because it is witty, because, again, the Woody persona has to use his wit to get out of a painful situation, which is the result of his sexual failure and even more of his failure in dealing with female sensibility (he was just wrongly ascribing Annie's bad mood to her period). Second, misunderstandings may be caused by homonyms and homophones (such as *Oedipus Wrecks/Oedipus Rex*); in our case the faked misunderstanding is based on a shift from the object level to the metalevel. Allen already dealt with this peculiar form of misunderstanding in one of his early texts (which, by the way, contain in germ many ideas of the later films). In "Spring Bulletin" we read: "Interesting aspects of stage history are also examined. For example, before the invention of italics, stage directions were often mistaken for dialogue, and great actors frequently found themselves saying, 'John rises, crosses left.' This naturally led to embarrassment and, on some occasions, dreadful notices. The phenomenon is analyzed in detail, and students are guided in avoiding mistakes."[42] It goes without saying that Allen here is making fun of professors' pedantry and not of actors' misunderstandings, as in *Annie Hall* he is making fun of a fundamental trait of Alvy—escaping from reality into art. His remark is witty, for the contrast between vulgar sexual problems and a work by James is huge, but it is, again, also funny: it fits Alvy to flee from Annie's (or Annie's and Alvy's?) sexual problems into the lofty sphere of literature—the act is, despite all external differences, fundamentally analogous to Andrew Hobbes's poetic flight through the air with Ariel to escape his sexual problems with Adrian (a flight ending with their plummeting into the lake) in *A Midsummer Night's Sex Comedy*. Third, the assertion that *My Sexual Problem* is the sequel of *The Turn of the Screw* is funny for two reasons. On the one hand, *screw* has a sexual meaning, and there is a certain, although limited, comic effect in interpreting one of the greatest American short stories, furthermore a masterpiece in horror, in this vulgar way. Such a witty misunderstanding is, however, not overwhelmingly comic, even if Shakespeare is full of analogous jokes—jokes, by the way, that have to be uttered very quickly if they are not to become unbearable, for they do not deserve too much attention; and indeed the tempo of Allen's films is usually *prestissimo* (*Scenes from a Mall* showing by its tempo alone that it was directed by someone else). On the other hand, in contrast to other sexual jokes, the idea that *The Turn of a Screw* has a sequel with the title *My Sexual Problem* does indeed deserve an afterthought; for Alvy as well as Allen—both having a tremendous knowledge of classical films, literature, and psychoanalysis—must be familiar with the psychoanalytic interpretation of the novel, which sees indeed sexual problems, namely hysteria, as the basis of the visions of the heroine, who very probably, if she had been brought up in a late modern cultural setting, would no longer see spirits but would instead discuss with her psychoanalyst her sexual attraction to the uncle of the children entrusted to her care and the transfer of this attraction to his nephew. The seemingly vulgar joke thus betrays a remarkable knowledge of the novel and its interpretations—the comic hero fleeing into the realm of literature is more competent than one might think.

The conversation between Alvy and Annie is framed and interrupted by the ongoing comments of an intellectual queuing behind them who is explaining in a loud voice to his companion the merits and demerits of Federico Fellini and Samuel Beckett. When he begins to name-drop Marshall McLuhan, Allen, who has shown his irritation to Annie in more and more aggressive terms, addresses both him and the audience of the film, claiming that the intellectual does not know anything about McLuhan's work. The man answers that he happens to teach a class on McLuhan at Columbia—so his insights into McLuhan must have a great deal of validity. In this situation Alvy claims to have McLuhan right there to back him up—and indeed McLuhan appears, played by himself (as, among others, in *Everything* Jack Barry, in *Zelig* Susan Sontag, Saul Bellow, and Bruno Bettelheim, in *Oedipus Wrecks* Edward Koch, in *Celebrity* Donald Trump, and in *Sweet and Lowdown* Woody Allen play themselves). McLuhan humiliates the man teaching his theory, even if he does so in a way that is intellectually not much more convincing than the remarks Alvy had to listen to before and therefore not at all didactic, but funny. Alvy then says to the audience: "Boy, if life were only like this!" The scene is fascinating not only because it breaks through the illusion the artwork creates (a strategy well known to Ancient Comedy as well as to Bertolt Brecht) but also because it contrasts Allen's intellectuality with that of the academic. Whereas the academic is arrogant, and his empty remarks have nothing to do with his own situation, Alvy identifies with artworks because they are linked to and can illuminate his problems, whether these are sexual or not, as in the case of Marcel Ophuls's *The Sorrow and the Pity* being linked to his Jewish identity and the moral problems surrounding the Holocaust. The Woody persona differs from the long gallery of artists, critics, producers, professors, and psychoanalysts depicted by Allen, not by avoiding being mediocre (many instantiations of him, though not all, are themselves obviously mediocre) but by having a childlike enthusiasm for ideals, for what is great in life and art. Ike's protest against Mary's and Yale's creation of the Academy of the Overrated (although his rage is an incipient sign of his attraction for Mary) redeems him, even if his remarks at the sculpture in the Whitney Museum are not much better than those of the young woman in front of the Jackson Pollock painting in *Play It Again, Sam.* But that he does not like average persons to declare Mahler or van Gogh overrated gives him a moral dignity that the self-appointed academy of the underraters does not have and that is probably a necessary, although not a sufficient, condition to become a really creative intellectual oneself. The greatest caricature of the empty academic is, of course, Leopold Sturgis in *Midsummer Night's Sex Comedy,* who has recently showed that "Balzac is overrated," defends a superficially rationalistic approach to reality, denies the existence of the spirit world, and, finally, overwhelmed by his repressed sexual desires, dies during sex and becomes a spirit himself. Sturgis's philosophy seems to be close to logical positivism (even if he combines it with a broad education in the arts), and indeed Allen makes it very clear that he does not have much respect for the rejection of the traditional metaphysical questions by many schools of analytical philosophy. When the extraterrestrial Og in *Stardust Memories* reacts to Sandy's questions of why there is so much human suffering and whether there is a God with the remarks that this is unanswerable and that these are the wrong questions, we remain unconvinced, despite Og's IQ of 1600, and we support Sandy's ongoing quest for meaning. Not that the Woody persona has any answers, but the mere fact that he continues to ask the right questions makes him fully human and therefore special. This is also true of his refusal to evade his own mortality and to be satisfied by the old Epicurean answer that we should not fear death, for as long as we are, death is not, and when death is, we are not—an idea present in the remarks of Mickey Sachs's old father to his son. Alvy's presents to Annie are *Death and Western Thought* and *The Denial of Death*, seemingly unfitting between lovers (and the first things to be returned after the split), but in the metaphysics of the Woody persona the experiences of love and death are interwoven: we are so interested in love because only love may give us the strength to face our mortality and overcome our fear of it. (This is at least Jake Fishbein's interpretation of the story told in "The Shallowest Man,"[43] and although it is not the only interpretation it is one of the best.) "Maybe the poets are right. Maybe love is the only answer," ruminates Mickey in *Hannah and Her Sisters*.[44]

Although not academic, the Woody persona is thus essentially an intellectual. In as early a film as *Take the Money and Run*, the criminal Virgil Starkwell shows his belief in the power of the word when he tries to rob a bank with the help of a written note—a note, though, so badly written that *gun* is read by the employees as *gub* and causes long hermeneutical discussions up to the vice president. His attempt to flee from prison with a pistol carved out of a bar of soap that then gets sudsy in the rain demonstrates again his trust in form over matter. Together with the director Fritz (an homage to Fritz Lang, whose *M* Allen will imitate in *Shadows and Fog*), Virgil plans to rob a bank by pretending to shoot a film about robbing a bank; the theme of trying to master life with the help of art will return in subtler forms in Allen's later films. When during the bank robbery by his gang another group of gangsters shows up with the same intent, he asks the customers to choose by whom they prefer to be robbed. Virgil is unable to commit himself to pure violence, which remains hemmed in by words and forms—he lacks the primitive vitality a gangster needs and therefore never makes the ten most wanted list. His wife complains about unfair voting—"it's who you know"— but the painful truth remains: even as a criminal the Woody persona is a failure, a schlemiel.

This is indeed one of his most crucial traits—the Woody persona mostly fails.[45] This lack of success is due not primarily to external causes; it has to do with the structure described in Alvy's aforementioned jokes and called by him "anhedonia" (which was originally intended as the title of what became *Annie Hall*)— that is, the incapacity to enjoy life. Fundamentally the Woody persona fears success and happiness, as represented, for example, by family life, because that would make him like the others, and even if he longs for happiness and integration, he knows that it would destroy his peculiar identity (which in its refusal to blend in with the environment is profoundly Jewish and, paradoxically in the case of Allen, culminates in the rejection of a traditional Jewish identity). As with a logical antinomy, this means that his failure is his success, because on a more profound level it is exactly what he needs—as in the case of Don Quixote. Alvy has lost Annie, whom he loved—but at the end he enjoys a "personal triumph": he sees Annie dragging her current boyfriend into Marcel Ophuls's film, which he taught her to love. The triumph is, to say the least, ambivalent, because it is linked to the perception that Annie has a new partner, while he is still alone; but probably, from his first remarks on the emerging aesthetics of photography onwards, Alvy wanted to educate her aesthetically at least as much as to be loved by her. Similarly in *Play It Again, Sam,* Allan loses Linda as a lover but simultaneously fulfills his most audacious dreams—to renounce her in a way that allows him to identify with Humphrey Bogart's behavior in the last scene of Michael Curtiz's *Casablanca,* which he was admiring when the film began (even if Linda is in any case determined to go back to Dick). After having said to Linda Rick's final lines to Ilsa in *Casablanca* and having enjoyed Linda's admiration, Allan confesses where his speech is from and says he has waited his whole life just to say it. Of course, the end of the movie is one of the most positive in Allen's whole production, insofar as the comic hero succeeds in freeing himself from his superego by imitating him where he ought to be imitated, namely in making the right moral decision. The film ends with the hope that Allan now has become so mature that he may finally engage in a substantial relationship, but whereas the play ended with a scene where Allan met a promising young woman and was able to speak with scientific objectivity about Bogart, the film (directed by Herbert Ross, with Allen's screenplay) remains in the aura of *Casablanca:* Allan walking alone on the airport field, enjoying his newly conquered autonomy from his model precisely by behaving like his model, only more lonely and therefore more heroic than Rick— for Rick lost Ilsa but at least gained the friendship of Capt. Renault.

Another difference between Allan and Rick is obvious: the great political context is missing. Mary Nichols has argued that the point of the film is that the virtues of honesty and friendship are important at all times, not only in exceptional times like World War II.[46] This is certainly true both in itself and as an interpretation of the film, but one must add that Rick's feeling that personal problems have little importance compared with the historical combat going on is difficult to maintain in the face of the demise of the political so manifest after the collapse of the totalitarian menace. The Woody persona is essentially a loner. It is true that at least at the beginning of his career he is endowed with a strong sense of friendship (which explains why he draws back from Linda). But as early as in *Manhattan* the Woody persona is confronted with a friend who snatches away from him the same girlfriend that he previously asked Woody to take over; and from a figure like Harry Block one could certainly expect similar behavior (even if the Woody persona is far more brutal toward women than toward men). As for the political dimension, it is clear that the Woody persona has no interest in it. *Bananas* and *Sleeper* are not counterexamples, for in them politics is only the background for the somehow megalomaniac romantic attempt to save the world through an action for, or with, the beloved one, even if *Sleeper* shares features of the antiutopias of our century, particularly Aldous Huxley's *Brave New World.* The dictator of San Marcos, Vargas, is repellent, but his revolutionary successor, Esposito, is even worse—he has to be eliminated too; and the new leader, Fielding himself, soon leaves the country for the United States, where he remains. Analogously, in *Sleeper* Miles fears, after the successful revolution by Erno, that in six months a new revolution will be necessary. Probably

Woody Allen is fundamentally apolitical, in the sense that he is interested mainly in individuals and moral choices and not in complicated institutional practices and visions.[47] This is compatible with his attacks against politicians he dislikes (such as both Nixon and Reagan in *Sleeper*) and even with scattered insights into some of the real problems of politics: when the new president Esposito introduces Swedish as the official language, one thinks of the necessary failure of revolutionary politics out of tune with local traditions in so many developing countries.

What about the religious dimension? Not only is *Love and Death* a parody of Russian literature of the nineteenth century, mainly of Tolstoy's *War and Peace;* it is also full of allusions to Bergman's *The Seventh Seal,* the film Allen in an interview once declared the best ever.[48] Both Antonius Block and Boris are looking for signs that prove the existence of God (Boris exemplifying them with a burning bush or Uncle Sasha picking up a check), both are confronted with death and encounter Death, and the films end with the heroes disappearing in a danse macabre. Boris has, of course, not only religious but also erotic problems (connected by his desire to know whether after death there are girls); and even if, because of the great probability that he will not survive a duel, he finally gets the promise of his beloved Sonja to marry him and she has to maintain her word, their marriage and their erotic relations are not described as ideal—as little as those of Fielding and Nancy are when he finally manages to marry her. Even more ambivalent than the erotic is Boris's religious experience. Expecting execution for a crime he did not commit, he finally gets the sign from God for which he has longed all his life. An angel tells him that he will be pardoned. But the angel lies, and he is shot.

Nevertheless, this religious disappointment is not a complete disaster. Boris is given the possibility of making a last communication after he has died—like other persons in the movie, but while those were concerned with very mundane matters (such as getting receipts for tax purposes), Boris alone manages to include in his last words something substantial (before he gets to sex). "The important thing, I think, is not to be bitter. If it turns out that there is a God, I don't think that he's evil. But the worst you can say about him is that basically he's an underachiever." This remark seems disrespectful, but it comes very close to ideas by philosophical theologians like Hans Jonas who think that if we have to choose between God's omnipotence or his goodness, we should certainly give up omnipotence but never the moral predicates of God. And by claiming that God is an underachiever the Woody persona, who is himself one, gets a chance to identify with him of which he would otherwise be deprived. Perhaps this is the reason for the exhilarating serenity of the dance in which Boris, leading Death (who is shrouded in white), takes leave of the world and the public. His final failure becomes a triumph— as in the case of Sid Waterman in *Scoop*. He is deceased, but he refuses to be discouraged.

Of course some manifestations of the Woody persona succeed in becoming happy; but in most cases there is an ironic reservation about these happy endings, mostly consisting in finding love, which is usually embedded in a larger context. Zelig becomes a stable personality at the side of Eudora Fletcher, but he dies young and without having finished reading *Moby Dick*. Danny Rose, the least narcissistic and most caring avatar of the Woody persona (who never assumes evil forms but sometimes assumes despicable ones), gets reconciled with Tina Vitale (one is not told explicitly whether something more develops); but we hear as the greatest glory of this holy man and patron saint of one-legged tap dancers, one-armed jugglers, and blind xylophone players that a sandwich was named after him. Nick Fifer and his wife decide to forgive each other their adulteries, but the bickering goes on. Kleinman overcomes his slavish subjection to others and decides to join the circus, but in the last image he disappears with the magician. Lenny Winerib saves his marriage and becomes a loving foster father, but he does not know that he himself has procreated a child—a normal paternity within a stable marriage is usually denied to the Woody persona. Larry Lipton owes the continuation of his marriage to a murder whose discovery brings the couple together. Andrew Hobbes finds his way back to his wife owing to a magic night in which supernatural elements play a role, but he has to renounce his earlier love for Ariel. The film with the most positive ending for the Woody persona and in general one of his warmest works is *Hannah and Her Sisters,* where Mickey Sachs not only remarries but becomes, surprisingly enough, a father—but after having gone through an attempted suicide.

The most striking feature of the Woody persona is of course his obsession with sex. But Woody is not simply lecherous, like Fritz Fassbender in *What's New, Pussycat?,* and the director Allen was, at least until *Deconstructing Harry,* almost prudish in his imagery, which avoided nudity. Allen's as well as Woody's interest in sex is, on the one hand, almost intellectual, based fundamentally on curiosity and on the irrevocable determination to overcome Woody's strong sexual inhibitions; on the other hand, it is subservient to a romantic ideal of love that is probably more burdened than enriched by the sexual dimension. The antinomic structure of the Woody persona—that he can accept love only from those persons who do not like him in an immediate or natural way—is the reason why he is attracted to neurotic women who spell trouble,[49] and since they seem to have the same attitude that he does, it explains why the Woody persona is so seductive for a certain type of woman. "But the greatest paradox of all is that ugly Woody, with his crooked face that only a Jewish mother could love, is deeply sexual, and decidedly cute. When they voted him one of the ten sexiest men in the country, the editors of *Playgirl* magazine claimed that he has "done more than anyone else to sexualize neuroticism."[50] One could say that while one of the origins of Greek comedy was the *phallagogia* and the actors of the Ancient Comedy continued to be adorned with leathery phalloi, the Woody persona blatantly exhibits his erection problems. The *vis comica* of Woody's sexual jokes usually does not stem from the circumvention of repression à la Freud; for in such jokes the sexual meaning usually appears suddenly and camouflaged at the end. Allen, in contrast, dealing with the god of the late twentieth century, namely sex, often uses the strategy of deflation normally dedicated to the subversion of metaphysical concepts: he begins with something sexual and takes the sexual tension away. His effect is therefore antipornographic. Allan Felix speaks of his honeymoon with Nancy, who has just left him—"spent the entire two weeks in bed. I had dysentery." And Cliff Stern tells his wife that he can remember the exact date when they had sex the last time, even though it was long ago—for it was Hitler's birthday. When Ike, provoked by Mary's comment that her dachshund is her penis substitute, responds that he would have expected in her case a Great Dane, it is not he who is obscene; he makes fun of *her* obscenity, besides showing remarkable psychological perspicacity. It is a popular source of the comic to show how men and women engage in intellectual conversations with the main end of finding out whether they want to go to bed with each other—an exchange of ideas preparing an exchange of fluids, as Cliff says in *Crimes and Misdemeanors*. But it is even more humorous when Alvy engages in a long political discussion with Allison because he does *not* want to have sex with her. Reflexes are funny in a half-Bergsonian sense—they are mechanisms of life. But when Alvy sneezes away cocaine whose price is about two thousand dollars an ounce, we laugh not so much at him as at the hosts' loss; what is subverted is the obsession with drugs, as the obsession with sex is subverted in other films.

In few spheres are compensation mechanisms as powerful as in the sexual, and therefore the Woody persona—beginning with Jimmy Bond—oscillates between megalomaniac ambitions and utter failure. Even Danny Rose, the good and modest Danny Rose, when asked whether he is married, answers: "No. I was engaged once to a dancer, you know, but, uh . . . she ran away with a piano player and I broke off with her."[51] Allan Felix daydreams before his first date that he will satisfy sexually not only the girl he is expecting and presumes frigid but all her frigid friends, too, although he has always frustrated his wife and will deter this girl and other women with his clumsiness (even the self-declared nymphomaniac Jennifer rejects his too-direct approach, which he, not wrongly, thought she provoked). It is a good addition in the film vis-à-vis the play that toward the end we finally see Nancy, Allan's ex-wife, and discover that she is quite different from the sexual vamp that appeared in

Allan's fantasies—they were simply not objective, being the constructions of an inhibited person feeling guilty. Sexual inhibition has in general a remarkable comic potential—from the scene in *Bananas* where Fielding buys the magazine *Orgasm,* which he tries to hide among respectable publications, and Lenny Winerib's first encounter with Linda in *Mighty Aphrodite* to Adrian's and Robin's visits to Dulcy and the hooker in *A Midsummer Night's Sex Comedy* and in *Celebrity* respectively. But techniques or desires cannot liberate people from their sexual inhibitions; the only thing that can accomplish this is the magical world of a midsummer's night, in which spirits help humans to become one with nature again—with all its attendant risks such as outbursts of primitive violence and premature death from too much exertion during sex.

Sexuality is also comic because it exemplifies a Bergsonian structure: it is a prerational, vital force, and every interference of reason or reflexivity as well as habitualization, inevitable in marriage, can prevent its proper function. Sexual artifices, as often envisaged by the Woody persona, are a sign that something is wrong, for there are no techniques to make one spontaneous; and, again, the effect is antipornographic when in episode 7 of *Everything* we observe the technical efforts that go on in the male body during orgasm. The switch to the interior of the body has immediate predecessors in science fiction movies, but it goes back at least to Rabelais, and in both cases it leads to a deflation, even a confounding of our expectations. (It shows furthermore that by going within the body we do not access the interior, subjective dimension—to express that, as in the outside world, the facial expressions of the technicians working inside the body are needed.) The activities of Dr. Bernardo in episode

6 of *Everything* are even grotesque—notwithstanding his success in having procured for hunchback Igor a four-hour orgasm, which produced his deformed shape. No less bizarre is the opposite idea that the sexual act should be so explosive that in a few minutes everything should be over— as suggested by the time the clock shows before and after the sexual encounter of Boris and Countess Alexandrovna, which leaves their bedroom in complete chaos. Obviously, not only self-perception but also a consideration of the expectations of the sexual partner and of society in general can endanger normal sexuality and lead to faking a pleasure one does not really feel. Erotic fantasies differ from individual to individual; and the greatest desire may be that the lover should be able to guess one's most hidden secrets. Few scenes in Allen are as comic as when Joe Berlin in *Everyone Says I Love You,* armed by an accidental knowledge of Von's sexual fantasies she has confessed to her analyst, whom his daughter has overheard, approaches her in Venice. The contrast between Joe's inhibition and his tremendous effort to overcome it when he begins to speak about Tintoretto, Von's favorite painter, whose existence he ignored till the day before, when he brings her a Gerbera, her favorite flower, and when he blows upon her back, fulfilling her most secret sexual fantasy, and Von's ecstatic reaction that she now must have found a magic person, the man of her dreams, is simply superb, and one has to be thankful to Allen for having recycled the idea of overhearing a conversation, which in *Another Woman* plays such a different role. Of course, the comic contrast is also so funny because it shows how much of the phenomenon of erotic attraction is a subjective construction—Von would only need to take a better look at Joe to know that he cannot be an erotic wizard. And

in fact, reality quickly dissipates this attraction —Von leaves her husband for Joe but returns to her husband after a few days.

Not only sex, however, but also the search for the perfect partner, whether for oneself or for another person, cannot be successfully undertaken in a conscious way. All the arranged dates for Allan Felix fail, and the arranger, Linda, and Allan fall in love. Hannah's attempts to find interesting single men for her sister Holly are hopeless, whereas Holly finally marries Hannah's former husband, whom she runs into by accident, a man who takes her seriously in a way Hannah never did, and the third sister, Lee, is having an affair with Hannah's current husband. Lenny Winerib in *Mighty Aphrodite* begins to become interested in Linda himself after he has found a mate for her—Kevin, who proves a complete failure. Nevertheless, Lenny's attempt to play God was not in vain— for on the way back from seeing Kevin, Linda finds a helicopter pilot who will become the right partner for her. Of course, this appearance of a deus ex machina from above is an ironic quotation from *What's New, Pussycat?* (Allen can now afford to quote himself instead of others) and has the function of showing the power of luck in erotic relations; but one has to recognize that Linda would not have been able to fascinate the pilot if she hadn't experienced Lenny's care and thereby matured.

But even if the Woody persona is ugly, shy, burdened with sexual problems, and unable to defend the courted woman from stronger males, even if Alvy is one of the few males suffering from penis envy and Ike is left by his wife for a woman, women do fall in love with him—as Linda does with Allan, as Betty Ann Fitzgerald does with CW Briggs, whom she seemed to hate so much and whom she reproached with "fragile masculinity," which CW in his answer calls his "religion" (a religion that proves attractive even to the millionaire Laura Kensington). Why? It is far too superficial to answer that the busy Dick neglects Linda—Linda begins to love Allan because she thinks that he, and not Dick, needs her. It is one of the paradoxes of power that in love relations weakness may be a power factor—for the weak person engenders the desire to protect and to help and may paralyze the capacity to use one's strength.[52] This structure has been analyzed already by Nietzsche, but for him the power of weakness, in the case of heterosexual relations, always belongs to the female sex. It is a result of the emancipation process, which, together with the sexual revolution, has altered gender relations in a way unheard of in human history, that the reverse has also become possible: on the one hand, there are strong women who may be felt, at least temporarily, as a burden by their partner and their family (like Hannah in *Hannah and Her Sisters*); on the other hand, the weaker man who confesses in a self-deprecatory manner both his penis envy and his masturbation (as a form of sex with someone he at least is sure to love) to his girlfriend may become attractive because he suggests to the bold woman the noble task of redeeming him, perhaps of transforming him into a hero, and of thereby solving her own identity problems. This ideal is a romantic one, and the Woody persona and his partners are indeed hopelessly romantic, even "neurotic romanticism's" greatest artistic expression. But it is a romanticism that has lost any belief in the sanctity of marriage (now regarded as the death of hope) and in classical gender roles; and it is not difficult to predict that such a romanticism, enlightened by self-help sex books and psychoanalysis, will be vexed, precarious, and prone to cynicism.

Tess represents common sense when she says to her sister Bea in *Radio Days* that she has to settle for something less than perfect if she wants to marry and become a mother, reminding Bea of preromantic times when a wife was just another mule. But even if Allen depicts the institution of the three-generation family in this most elegiac film of his with affection and nostalgia (few relations are as touching as that of Joe to his father, who both spanks and loves him and whom Joe finally discovers to work as a cabdriver), he knows that it is gone forever in our world, as the radio days have gone. In *Husbands and Wives* Jack and Sally reconcile after separation because they value enough what they have from each other even if they would wish for more, while Gabe and Judy, whose shock at the news of their friends' separation betrayed that they were secretly considering divorce themselves (their feelings being accentuated by a jump-cut technique reminiscent of Jean-Luc Godard), leave each other. Gabe is superficially involved with Rain, whose personality type is repeated by Nola in *Celebrity,* a type with whom a lasting relationship is obviously impossible. But Lee Simon leaves a hopeful relationship for trouble with Nola, and although his behavior is despicable, one feels a certain compassion even for him, a man whose midlife-crisis ambitions with regard to his life all fail miserably while Robin, the wife he repudiated in order to realize them, thereby manages to become a successful show business personality, even if she despises her new job. We pity Lee somehow, for he is a victim of the delusions connected with romanticism, which have vexed many persons for the last two hundred years.

The Woody persona will continue to desire a woman who is both sexually and intellectually challenging and satisfying, although in the depth of his soul he knows that if both criteria could be simultaneously satisfied he would become bored, long for variety, and begin to look for another woman. In "The Lunatic's Tale" the surgeon transplants the brain of his very intelligent partner Olive Chomsky into the body of the erotic archetype Tiffany. The operation succeeds, but "after several months of bliss with Olive that was the equal of anything in the *Arabian Nights*, I inexplicably grew dissatisfied with this dream woman and developed instead a crush on Billie Jean Zapruder, an airline stewardess whose boyish, flat figure and Alabama twang caused my heart to do flip-flops."[53] In one of the films by Sandy Bates shown in *Stardust Memories* an analogous operation is performed on Doris and Rita, and the surgeon played by Sandy confesses: "So, I performed the operation and everything went perfectly. I-I-I switched their personalities and I took all the badness and put it over there. And I made Rita into a warm, wonderful, charming, sexy, sweet, giving, mature woman. And then I fell in love with Doris."[54]

The Great Philosophical Issues in Allen's Movies

In his interview with Stig Björkman Allen states that of the persons he created the ones he has most identified with are not necessarily just the various versions of the Woody persona (among his avatars he seemed to prefer Alvy Singer) but also other, increasingly female figures as well—particularly Eve, the mother in *Interiors,* with her cold search for aesthetic perfection.[55] It is indeed obvious that

Allen the director does not fail and that to succeed he must have certain qualities the Woody persona lacks. But despite his obsession with technical quality Allen shares one concern with the Woody persona—an interest in the great philosophical and theological questions. This is why he feels very close to Russian literature: "I don't think that one can aim more deeply than at the so-called existentialist themes, the spiritual themes. That's probably why I'd consider the Russian novelists as greater than other novelists. Even though Flaubert, for example, is a much more skilled writer than, I think, either Dostoyevsky or Tolstoy . . . his work can never be as great, for me, personally, as the other two."[56] Perhaps this explains why Allen's movie *Love and Death,* which made the transition from his earlier, more slapstick-like comedies to the more reflective and organic ones, is a parody of Russian literature and why this work is full of allusions to philosophical figures and arguments. But Sonja's comparison of various leaves in order to find that they are all different (like that of the princesses introduced by Leibniz to the principle of identity of indiscernibles) and her discussion of a familiar (and misleading) objection to the categorical imperative ("If everyone went to the same restaurant and ordered blintzes there'd be chaos")[57] are associative and not really linked to one main philosophical issue, in contrast to Boris's execution for a crime he did not commit, which can be seen as a parable of the human condition. The later films become much more focused on single philosophical issues, and even if they are great films only because the relation between image, music, and text is extremely elaborate, and the scripts are excellent only because the nature of human beings as well as the way they communicate with each other is rendered with utmost precision, here I can deal merely with the philosophy that emerges from these films. Allen's psychology has to be ignored as well, even though it too certainly deserves a thorough analysis: his splendid insights concern the "microeconomics" of human relations, gender relations and increasingly the relations within a family, between parents and children as well as between siblings, relations that, as Louis Levy teaches in *Crimes and Misdemeanors,* significantly determine one's later erotic relations. Insights into the "macroeconomics" of human relations, into the way, for example, political power works, are hardly to be found in Allen: he remains faithful to the limitation of comedy, from the New Comedy onwards, to topics that do not concern the highest, the ruling classes, whose problems are reserved for tragedy. The only tragedies Allen knows are, as in Chekhov, private, never public tragedies, even if in *Match Point* and *Scoop* the nature of a class society is depicted with merciless realism.

What are Allen's philosophical problems? His starting point is the existentialist concept of authenticity. His heroes are obliged to be themselves—even Danny Rose is "currently working with a parrot that sings 'I Gotta Be Me'" (the point being that even entities without any possibility of being themselves can be trained to say they are longing for authenticity).[58] Now, it is not easy for the philosopher to explain what this concept means. Since Heidegger we know that it at least entails facing one's mortality, and sadness, implicit in the distance between the young Joe, played by Seth Green, and the old voice of the aged narrator, Allen's own, is the price that we have to pay for our knowledge of our temporality and our effort to overcome it by the work of memory (*Radio Days* being such a work, comparable to Fellini's *Amarcord*). It is certainly even more difficult to live authenticity, if it implies that one is not allowed to follow role models, including the traditional source of normativity, God ("I-I gotta model myself after someone," exclaims Ike when Yale, rightly criticized, reproaches him for being self-righteous and behaving like God). Most of the persons in Allen's universe who claim to be original are nothing more than functions of the spirit of their time, sharing its most vulgar aspects. The subtle power of the media that undermine all potential authentic feelings by claiming to mirror them is from the beginning one of Allen's major issues, particularly of course in *Bananas,* where presidents dying as victims of a coup as well as young spouses after their first night are exhorted to share their experiences with the camera, and in *Everything,* where people participate in a TV quiz "What's My Perversion?" Nevertheless Allen believes that there is no way to avoid the duty to become oneself, as even his small-time crooks Ray and Frenchy Winkler understand at the end of their futile attempt to gain an education corresponding to their new wealth. Allan Felix has to free himself from the overpowering model of Bogart to become a normal human being. We have already seen that the end of the film is profoundly ambivalent: Allan does not need Bogart any more and understands that the secret is to be no longer Bogart but himself. However, his determination to be authentic is represented in an exaggeration of the Bogartian mood. On the one hand, this is unavoidable—for Allan owes Bogart much indeed, and the model for which Rick stands must not be relinquished. On the other hand, in the film version it cannot be excluded that Allan, determined to no longer ape the virility that fitted Bogart but not him, will imitate the ideal of the loner.

The role of Howard Prince that Allen played in Martin Ritt's *The Front* also has to do with the problem of borrowed identity. Passing himself off as the author of the scripts of the blacklisted Al Miller, Howard conquers Florence Barrett; but he can gain authenticity only by finally joining the political struggle and being jailed for it. Howard is not only a successor of Christian de Neuvillette in Edmond Rostand's *Cyrano de Bergerac,* a work also remarkable for its combination of tragic and comic features, but also a predecessor of David Shayne in *Bullets over Broadway.* A mediocre writer, David has success with his drama only because the text is rewritten by Cheech, the bodyguard who must protect Olive, the awful actress and lover of the Mafia boss Nick Valenti, who sponsors the play under the condition that Olive act in it. One can argue that Cheech is the real hero of the film. But David, who had been convinced by his agent to accept every humiliation, gains dignity when he recognizes that he cannot build his career on a lie and further that he is not talented enough for art, lacking, among other things, the willingness to kill and be killed for it. He relinquishes his literary ambitions as well as his infatuation for the aging star Helen Sinclair and marries his girlfriend Ellen. Ellen in turn breaks with the cynical intellectual Sheldon Flender, who consoled her while David had his affair with Helen. Becoming a husband and hopefully a father, David redefines himself; and even if his self-image may have become more modest, he can claim finally to have found, as did Cheech in his own way, authenticity (which other untalented people in Allen's universe, such as Peter in *September,* lack because they are not able to recognize their shortcomings). Emmet Ray in *Sweet and Lowdown,* the counterfigure to David, is a great guitarist and a brutal, even if vulnerable man; his temporary girlfriend Hattie cannot speak but is able to feel the emotions Emmet expresses only in his art, not in his life. Emmet knows himself to be second only to Django Reinhart, whose superiority threatens his identity. It is impossible not to interpret the film reflexively: Allen speaks about his own relationship to Federico Fellini, whose *La Strada* is the clear model of *Sweet and Lowdown.*

Of course the most tormented search for authenticity is represented by Leonard Zelig. The technical perfection of this pseudodocumentary (a form already tried in *Take the Money and Run* and repeated in *Sweet and Lowdown*) has, as Allen complained, "obscured the points he was trying to make about a man afraid to be himself."[59] But it is exactly because of the technical qualities of Allen's film that Zelig has become one of the most impressive icons of the twentieth century. *The Purple Rose of Cairo* is the richer and more complex movie, but the transition from normal reality to the ontologically different sphere of the contents of an artwork has been thematized several times before—it plays a central role in Luigi Pirandello's work. The chameleon man, however, is an absolutely original creation, congenial, furthermore, to the medium of film—a painting could not show the change, a book could not make it visible. The choice of the documentary form is not only determined by the obvious difficulties of making a nondocumentary film about a man who turns fat or black, for example, whenever he stands close to such a person; as in *Broadway Danny Rose,* the frame allows the comic hero to gain an almost mythic stature. (Since the frame in *Zelig* is in color, the documented world appears to be very distant from the present.) And the documentary makes it possible to combine the story of an individual with the picture of an age—the 1920s and 1930s, which indeed witnessed, after the crash of the old order in the First World War, one of the greatest identity crises in human history and the false attempts to overcome it through totalitarianism. *Zelig* can even be compared with Thomas Mann's fictitious biography *Doctor Faustus* (which includes historical persons, too, in order to maintain the appearance of objectivity), since in both works the fate of an individual and of a political culture are skillfully interwoven. But while in Mann the person whose life is described is extraordinary because of his genius and concomitant guilt over sacrificing everything to it (so that the novel runs the risk of mythologizing national socialism), Zelig is paradoxically uncommon only because he is an Everyman wanting to be like the others to a degree hitherto unknown.

As always in Allen, the basis of the political dimension is a personal problem. Zelig's exorbitant chameleonic powers with regard to his exterior are only the expansion of a feature most humans have—that they adapt their opinions to those of their environment, and this often not for strategic reasons but with subjective sincerity. The first recorded appearance of Zelig is of such a nature: Scott Fitzgerald meets a man who extols in an upper-class Boston accent the Republican Party and the rich when he speaks with socialites and declares himself one hour later in a coarse accent a Democrat when talking to the kitchen help. Later on Zelig confesses that his adaptive capacities emerged first in school when he answered some very bright people's question as to whether he had read *Moby Dick* in the affirmative, even though he had never read it.[60] This type of dishonesty, so common among intellectuals, is a sign of lacking authenticity—Zelig is unable to admit his own shortcomings. As it becomes clear, Zelig's morbid desire to be like others is based on the lack of love he experienced as a child: one does indeed learn to hate Zelig's family when the small progress the psychiatrist Eudora Fletcher makes at the beginning with regard to the diagnosis of his disease is interrupted by his half-sister, Ruth, and her lover with the ironic name Martin Geist, who seize the occasion of Zelig's becoming famous to tour the world with him in order to make money. Through them Zelig becomes, despite all his social successes, like John Merrick in David Lynch's film *Elephant Man,* a freak instrumentalized by greedy and curious persons. Like Frederick Treves, the doctor who redeems Merrick, Eudora Fletcher is determined "to bring out the human being behind Zelig's zombielike stare," but custody rights are with Ruth, and only the violent death of her and Martin Geist in Spain gives Eudora a second chance. First, however, the missing Zelig must be found, a task that proves difficult, if not impossible, until in the immediate vicinity of Pope Pius XI during the Easter blessing on Rome a disturbing figure is seen. The *vis comica* of this scene is overwhelming, for obviously Zelig's chameleonlike nature threatens to bring back the time of the antipopes: one can bear an additional physician but hardly an additional pope. Zelig's appearance in the Vatican is the first sign of his attraction to a system that limits and thereby supports the individual, but Allen not only insinuates that Roman Catholicism ranges somehow between American individualism and German national socialism but also recognizes the huge differences between the two places where Zelig takes refuge: the pope tries only to swat the intruder, who is then returned to the United States by Italian authorities, whereas the Nazis want to torture and kill him.

Even in the beginning, Eudora rejected the naturalistic approach her colleagues took with regard to the Zelig phenomenon—Dr. Birsky, for example, assumed that Zelig had a brain tumor, but as the narrator's voice-over tells us, ironically enough, it is Dr. Birsky himself who within two weeks dies of a brain tumor. Dr. Birsky's crude naturalistic approach is similar to that of the doctor in *Shadows and Fog* who hopes to solve the problem of evil by dissecting brains and to that of the camera reporter in *The Purple Rose of Cairo* who says that the phenomenon of Tom Baxter's leaving the screen can be explained by electrical storms in the air. But Eudora's original method is also doomed to fail: even if she does not believe in a physiological explanation of the Zelig phenomenon, she objectifies her patient. She exemplifies Habermas's point that psychoanalysis and ideology critique have an intermediate position between the natural sciences and hermeneutic efforts. Zelig defends himself against her paternalistic approach by behaving like a psychiatrist himself: he tells her that he is "treating two sets of Siamese twins with split personalities. I'm getting paid by eight people."[61] (The multiple personality syndrome had interested William James and became popular in the United States through Nunnally Johnson's film *The Three Faces of Eve*.) Eudora's efforts to overcome his resistance are all in vain until she has a great idea: since she cannot work on him, she has to work with him. She shifts from an objectifying to a dialogic approach, taking his identity as a psychiatrist seriously. By purporting herself to have a problem, namely having been afraid of admitting that she had not read *Moby Dick*, she slowly gains Zelig's confidence, and when she pretends not to be a doctor and to need his advice, Zelig can finally recognize that he himself is not a doctor either. But the question "Who are you?" he cannot answer: "What do you mean who am I, I, I don't know. These are tough questions. . . . No, I'm nobody, I'm nothing."[62] Later he will begin to speak about his past, his violent family as well as that rabbi who, asked to tell him the meaning of life, did so, but unfortunately in Hebrew, which twelve-year-old Leonard did not understand—Kafka's parable in *The Trial* transformed into one of Allen's best jokes. When he is put in a trance and exhorted to speak about his real desires, he confesses, among other things, to being a Democrat and to hating Eudora's pancakes but to loving her personally because she is not as clever as she thinks she is. When he is in a normal state, Eudora, who liked him from the beginning and begins to fall in love with him, shows him the affection he had to try to get by adapting to his environment. With this treatment she manages to cure him: first she exaggerates her therapy by rendering Zelig too overopinionated, but finally she makes a normal person of him. The two become celebrities and are invited everywhere, a film shall be made of them, and they decide to marry. The story could finish here, proving that the solution to the identity problem is love but that one can love only if one has the courage to be oneself. (In *Another Woman* the point is more general; but similarly in that film Marion can gain authenticity, and thereby perhaps become able to relate in a more sincere and loving way to her environment, only through her encounter with Hope, with whom at the end she loses contact.)

But now several women appear, claiming Zelig has already married them. The tide turns—Zelig is rejected by the American public, and although Eudora remains loyal to him his desire to be loved by everybody once again makes him turn into bystanders and finally disappear for a second time.

Zelig is discovered after a long time by Eudora in a newsreel scene about Nazi Germany. She immediately travels to Berlin and finds Zelig finally in Munich, flanking Hitler during a speech at a rally. She manages to contact him, he interrupts Hitler, who was just making a joke about Poland, and both manage to flee, although pursued by the Nazis, steal a biplane, and fly back to America. The narrative strategies used to make this story plausible are simply superb: some of it is shown through a film within the film, "The Changing Man" of 1935, and in German and American newsreels of the time; some of it is reported in an interview with former SS Obergruppenführer Oswald Pohl; and all these sources are connected by the narrator's voice-over. Back in America, Zelig becomes a hero, solves his legal problems, and can finally marry Eudora.

The addition of this last part is important for at least four reasons. It shows, first, that the problem of the search for identity cannot be solved just in a dyad. Eudora's intelligence and, even more, her love have redeemed Zelig, but they do not prove sufficient to keep him sane; he also needs the recognition of his polity. Second, the last part throws at least as much light on national socialism as does *Doctor Faustus*. Saul Bellow's comments on why Zelig joined national socialism—"there was also something in him . . . that desired . . . immersion in the mass and . . . anonymity, and Fascism offered Zelig that kind of opportunity, so that he could make something anonymous of himself by belonging to this vast movement"[63]—capture probably more basic psychological presuppositions of fascism than Mann's reflections, even if in the peculiar version of German national socialism the desire to achieve something outstanding in world history also played an important role. Third, fleeing in the biplane from the Nazis, Eudora Fletcher, a good pilot, loses consciousness, and Zelig, who has never flown before, turns pilot himself: his chameleon disease saves them. From this final perspective, the disease no longer appears as merely negative and threatening; one has to go through identity disturbances to achieve something heroic. Finally, the last part gives Allen a chance to make clear in his film most dedicated to the topic of authenticity that the latter can be only a necessary, never a sufficient, condition of moral behavior—for in Hitler's speech that Zelig interrupts, ideals of autonomy play an important role (as in Martin Heidegger's philosophy): "Glaubt niemals an fremde Hilfe, niemals an Hilfe, die außerhalb unserer eigenen Nation, unseres eigenen Volkes liegt" (Never believe in foreign help, never believe in help that comes from outside our own nation and our own people). One of Allen's best jokes occurs in *Bananas* when Fielding mentions Kierkegaard in order to impress Nancy. "Oh, well, of course he's Danish," she responds, and Fielding hastens to remark, "He'd be the first to admit that." Probably Fielding does not know the meaning of "Danish" but believes it denotes some form of perversion; what solely counts for him, but not for Allen, is sincerity about it. It is extremely important to be oneself, but it is not enough. Freedom is a frightening thought, as we hear both in *Alice* and in *Manhattan Murder Mystery.*

But if authenticity is not, as the existentialists wrongly claimed, enough for a decent life, where do the further requisites come from? Before Tina Vitale succeeds in resolving to go to Danny Rose and apologize, she goes to Angelina to get her advice. But Angelina (who "once even predicted I would marry a Jew")[64] is not there—she is celebrating Thanksgiving with her grandchildren, and no insistence on Tina's part with regard to the importance of her visit can bring her back in time. Allen points out that Tina has to make her decision by herself (even if Robin's analogous decision to return to her groom is helped by the advice of the psychic, one of the few honest persons in *Celebrity*, it is still she who must know what she wants). Nevertheless, Tina is not completely alone when she dares enter the apartment of the man she betrayed—betrayed mainly through an omission, but still betrayed. Tina can quote his Uncle Sidney: "acceptance, forgiveness, and love." The elder relatives Danny keeps quoting are—despite their oddness—models, and even the authentic individual cannot live without models. In Allen's philosophy there are two, perhaps three realms that compete to fill the void that modern, authentic persons are confronted with: art, morality, and, within limits, religion. They all have the same function—to propose concrete contents without which even the authentic person is doomed to fail—but they don't all have the same value. It may seem surprising but Allen's evaluation of the three stages is close to that of Kierkegaard, the father of authenticity and the greatest philosopher of troublesome relations between man and woman: at least they agree in their conviction that art is only the first step. There is something moving in the fact that Allen, without a shadow of a doubt a great artist, is so skeptical with regard to the possibilities of art. This follows from Allen being, in the core of his personality, a moralist, an earnest moralist who chose comedy as the tool most fitting his natural talents to communicate his demanding and sad moral message. This message is that one ought to be moral even if there is no God. Morality for Allen, as for Kant, does not owe its validity to the existence of God, which seems to be in contradiction with the existence of human suffering and evil. "Just on a simplistic level. Why-why were there Nazis?"[65] But is there really no God? Has he been successfully murdered by an existentialist, as in Allen's story "Mr. Big,"[66] a parody of a detective story à la Dashiel Hammett's "The Maltese Falcon," where the detective finally discovers that the young woman who hired him to find out whether God really exists and with whom he falls in love is responsible herself for the brutal murder of God, who in the meantime has been delivered to the morgue? Was Zeus strangled when he tried to play the deus ex machina in a drama, as in Allen's extremely reflexive play *God*?[67] Is it really the author's message that "God is dead. Stop. You're on your own"?[68] Not only the fact that this message contradicts that of the play within the play (the character Diabetes brings the answer "yes" to the king's question—"my question of questions," "the only question"—whether there is a god—and is condemned to be torn apart by wild horses because the king fears that if there is a god he will be doomed for eternity), but also the facts that the author's message is brought by a delivery boy on a bicycle, who first reads the wrong telegram, and that it is signed by "The Moscowitz Billiard Ball Company" make us suspicious; furthermore, we remember the irony with which the author's message was highlighted in *What's New, Pussycat?* Perhaps Allen wants only to say that Zeus is not at home right now, as his answering machine tells us in *Mighty Aphrodite?* It seems clear that Allen is a tormented agnostic, but not an atheist: "To you I'm an atheist . . . to God I'm the loyal opposition."[69] On the one hand, he makes fun again and again of established religion, mainly his own but also other varieties (particularly Catholicism); on the other hand, he recognizes the support that rituals give to human life

(Thanksgiving is a crucial event both in *Broadway Danny Rose* and in *Hannah and Her Sisters*). This, however, does not solve the religious problem; for an atheist could also acknowledge the social importance of religion, which, in any case, for Allen as an existentialist is not central. But there are, as we will see, hints in Allen's work of metaphysical, and not only psychological or sociological, arguments in favor of God's existence.

Allen's criticism of art again and again becomes as severe as that of Plato, Kierkegaard, or Tolstoy. Of course, there is also some beautiful recognition of the positive function of art in his films, and one can partly ease the tension between the two types of assertions by relating them to different types of art. Radio permitted a participation of the audience and a form of community precluded to moviegoers and doubtless enriched the life of Joe's family and their generation. But this differentiation helps only partly. For even great art does not save humans from their mortality, and Chris Wilton's love for operas does not prevent him from becoming a murderer. *The Purple Rose of Cairo* is, like *Play It Again, Sam,* a movie about the function of films in life, and its answer is, unlike that of the earlier movie, fundamentally negative and depressing.[70] Art fosters escapism, and even if it may open up a world that is purer than reality, that ideal world cannot change the real one. Cecilia flees from the sadness of her marriage and of her work during the Depression into the world of the films representing the glittering life of the rich and happy, and even if her flight is nobler than that of her husband, Monk, who invites prostitutes home, its first consequence is that, being negligent at work due to discussions with her sister about the movies she has seen, Cecilia loses her job. But instead of changing her attitude, she goes again to the cinema, where she sees three times in succession a superficial film with the title "The Purple Rose of Cairo" that she has already seen twice. The title alludes, as the naive poet, adventurer, and explorer Tom Baxter, the most positive figure in the film, explains, to an old Egyptian legend: "A pharaoh had a rose painted purple for his queen, and now the story says . . . purple roses grow wild at her tomb."[71] And as the painted rose was able to transform itself into real ones, so the figure within the film, Tom Baxter, suddenly addresses Cecilia, whose long presence he has noticed, and leaves the screen. This extraordinary event has repercussions on three levels. First, the film cannot go on as usual. The other figures, unable to leave the screen themselves, engage in various discussions, partly with the public, some members of which are fascinated by the new situation; one of these, for example, is a student of the human personality who, as his wife says, has trouble with real people and turns to art as a compensation. But most of the public is upset, with the result, second, that the producers, who fear legal quarrels, feel obliged to react—especially since in other cities as well the Tom Baxter character shows an inclination to leave the screen. Consequently, they plan to bring Baxter back into the movie, then withdraw it and destroy the prints and the negative. The actor who played Tom Baxter, Gil Shepherd, understands that if he does not want to endanger his career he has to cooperate.

The third and most important immediate consequence is the romance between Cecilia and Tom. Tom, flattered by Cecilia's dedication and wishing to meet her, has left the film, but in general he feels a childlike curiosity with regard to the real world outside the film and desires to be free from his role. As the press agent says: "The real ones want their lives fiction, and the fictional ones want their lives real."[72] Tom is grateful to taste popcorn for the first time, as he has so often seen his audience eating it, and he convinces Cecilia, with whom he elopes from the cinema, to come back in the evening, despite her qualms concerning her duties toward Monk. But when Tom invites her to a supper club, he has only fake money and cannot pay, and he cannot even escape by car, since he does not have its key. This may explain why, when by chance the next day she meets Gil Shepherd, who has hurried to the place of the disaster (and whom, in a scene reminiscent of the classical twin comedies, she begins to address, to his utter surprise, as Tom), she is excited in a way that she wasn't when Tom came out from the screen. In a certain sense, Cecilia is more interested in the real glittering world the movie stars live in than in what they represent; and indeed Gil's claim that he created Tom—or, at least, fleshed him out—has a certain plausibility. Gil enjoys an ontological priority with regard to Tom, who is, furthermore, only *one* of his creatures—for Gil played also in "Honeymoon in Haiti," another of Cecilia's favorites, and is expected to play in the near future Charles Lindbergh. But the ontological priority does not match up with any moral priority—Tom is a sweet and innocent person sincerely in love with Cecilia, while Gil, a former cab driver whose real name is Herman Bardebedian, is vain, vulgar, false, and only interested in his career. In the first encounter between Tom and Gil, Gil insists that Cecilia cannot love Tom—he may be perfect, but he is not real, and "What good is 'perfect' if the man's not real?!"[73] The question reminds one of Gaunilo's objection to Anselm's ontological proof, even if Tom's perfection is obviously only a finite one, which in no case could entail existence. But Tom wants to learn to be real—even if Gil, the defender of reality, in a comparison disparaging reality as well as himself, objects: "Can't learn to be real. It's like learning to be a midget. It's not a thing you can learn. Some of us are real, some are not." Cecilia satisfies Tom's curiosity, teaching him in a poetic and wordless scene what pregnancy is and then bringing him to an empty church. Tom is not familiar with the concept of God, but he tries to make sense of Cecilia's vague explanation by identifying him with the two screenwriters of "The Purple Rose of Cairo" (not with Gil). Cecilia objects: "I'm talking about something much bigger than that. No, think for a minute. A reason for everything. Eh, otherwise, i-i-it-it'd be like a movie with no point, and no happy ending."[74] The joke is, of course, that God is without any doubt "bigger" than the screenwriters of a mediocre movie—if he exists; if not, the latter have the same advantage with regard to God as Gil has with regard to Tom. Tom is struck by the new concept, and it is fascinating to see that he very quickly shifts its meaning from an aesthetic to an ethical level, for when in the church he is attacked by the jealous Monk and manages to knock him down but, in trying to help him up, is overwhelmed by him, he cries: "God, it's not fair!" Despite his defeat, Tom is not hurt—his incarnation is only partial, in contrast with that of the Christian God, in whose temple the fight takes place, and this explains why Tom fails to transform reality. Cecilia is skeptical with regard to his capacity to survive off the screen if he continues to refuse to "fight dirty." And she is right—Monk's tricks are relatively clean compared to the activities of Gil, who continues to woo Cecilia and to bait her with promises to show her Hollywood in order to get control of Tom again. Meanwhile, Tom continues to muse about God and his relation to the screenwriters, about life in general, about death and childbirth and their magic—together with prostitutes who are profoundly touched by his speech (as they will be by Irmy's visit in *Shadows and Fog*). The real world changes, is full of risks, knows birth and death with its finality, and Tom longs for it—but, as Gil had anticipated, he cannot take root in it. Cecilia, who has defended Tom with the words "He's fictional, but you can't have everything," seems to regard his only fault as more and more disturbing: "Y-you're-you're some kind of phantom." And indeed, Tom cannot invite her into a real restaurant, but he has the idea to go back with her into the screen, where she joins him and the other movie figures in the Copacabana; afterwards he shows her the town. But now Gil appears in the cinema, and he exhorts Cecilia to leave the screen and come with him, saying that he loves her. Finally Cecilia decides against perfection and for reality—she leaves the screen and Tom and goes home to break with Monk in order to follow Gil. When she comes back to meet Gil, he is gone, and the "Purple Rose of Cairo" letters are taken from the marquee. She enters the cinema to see the new movie, with no other future but to return to Monk, who has told her: "You'll be back!" and no other recourse but to lose herself again in the celluloid worlds the cinema has to offer.

The central theme of the film is unreciprocated and sterile love. Tom loves Cecilia, but Cecilia loves him back only as long as she doesn't meet Gil, who turns her love away from Tom but does not reciprocate it. Neither of the two loves engenders anything. In more general terms, the real world longs for the ideal, but only as long as it leaves reality untouched and even educates one to apathy: the film industry must destroy a film that threatens to influence reality, Cecilia is unwilling and unable to find a form of existence that would allow her to live with a phantom, and Gil, despite his partial identity with Tom and his creation of a good person, is himself banal and fraudulent. As Plato said, art lies, and it is furthermore ontologically deficient. While in "The Kugelmass Episode" the protagonist, a humanities professor, is transported from the real world into an artwork (the novel *Madame Bovary*), the charm of the later film is that the ontological transition originates in the ideal world: it is the ideal world, or at least a part of it, that strives to become real because of its awe for existence. Paradoxically, this trait is rooted in the autonomy of the ideal world—Tom longs for existence because he is better than the existing world, which would like to keep him in the environment of socialites. But the desire of the ideal for the real is powerless. Tom may be able to leave the screen, but his whole existence is parasitic; he has to go back to the screen in order to invite his beloved to dinner.

What impact does Tom's appearance finally have on the world? Profound sadness in Cecilia (who must feel guilty, although in the long run she would have had to decide the same way again, even if she no longer trusted Gil), feelings of superiority in Monk, perhaps nostalgic memories in the prostitutes, are all that remains of this incarnation: *The Purple Rose of Cairo* is indeed a film without a happy ending, the world without God incarnate. The idea of a reciprocal transformation of the ideal by the real and of the real by the ideal, so important in the tradition of objective idealism (usually committed to the ontological proof), is alien to the film. Art does not lead to a better or fuller life, and life is not even mirrored by films such as "The Purple Rose of Cairo." Arnold W. Preussner has interpreted "the silver screen itself as a cinematic equivalent of the second or 'green world' of Shakespearean 'festive' comedy,"[75] but the decisive difference is that the encounter with the magic forest transforms the Shakespearean heroes (even if not always in a credible way), while the silver screen has no redeeming power. Rilke's "Du mußt dein Leben ändern" (You must change your life), an important verse in *Another Woman,* has no place in *The Purple Rose of Cairo.* One could, however, counter that this is a consequence of the low aesthetic value of "The Purple Rose of Cairo" (I mean the film within the film): even Tom in his lovely innocence is not a mature human being, so it makes perfect sense not to choose him as a partner for life, even setting aside the issue of his ontological status.

Allen's representation of art is somber, even when he deals with good art. In *Interiors,* a work in many ways similar to Henrik Ibsen's last drama, *When We Dead Awaken,* Eve has an excellent aesthetic sense for the decoration of houses, but what she constructs is an ice palace in which everything seems to be in harmony but in truth is suffocated. Her rival, Pearl, is vulgar, but her vulgarity allows for life. Eve's most gifted daughter, Renata, is a good poet but obsessed with herself and depressed by the clear consciousness that the immortality some of her poems might have is not at all a compensation for her own mortality.[76] But art is not only futile and oppressing—art can even lead to murders. Cheech in *Bullets over Broadway* is not only a professional killer with a high work ethic but also a naturally talented dramatist, and since he is unable to tolerate David's bad script he rewrites it. He does not have any ambition to be recognized as its author, for he loves art for art's sake, but he wants his work represented with due care. Therefore he eliminates that unfortunate successor to Sally White of

Radio Days, Olive, for whom he was hired as a bodyguard, because her poor acting ability dramatically lowers the quality of the performance. His behavior is risky, and in fact the godfather finds out the truth and has him killed during the performance of his play. The gunshots will be particularly praised by the reviewers, who mistake them as a part of the play: while in *The Purple Rose of Cairo* a part of the artwork enters reality, here (as in Luigi Pirandello's novella *The Bat*) it is reality that enters, at least in the perception of the public, the artwork. Cheech would not have liked this demolition of the autonomy of his artwork, since for him everything is subordinated to beauty. But Cheech is just in that he is willing to sacrifice his own life as well as that of others to achieve artistic perfection. In his last words to David he does not utter any complaint, but he suggests a great ending for the play: the heroine who in its first version was frigid should announce that she is pregnant (obviously an allusion to the end of *Hannah and Her Sisters*). Thereby Cheech shows that his ultimate concern is his artwork and nothing else; but by acknowledging the artistic importance of birth he unconsciously recognizes that art ultimately relies on life. David's decision to give up art and found a family is the type of reality even art needs. Cheech has a certain greatness owing to his consistency and artistic abilities, while the intellectual Flender is only ridiculous because he develops theories similar to those of Cheech but is not able to act like him—he can only betray his friend David by seducing his fiancée. Flender likes to discuss moral dilemmas such as whether one should save from a burning house the last copy of Shakespeare's plays or a human being and teaches that the artist creates his own moral universe. Obviously, Flender's theory destroys any objectivity of morality and opens the door to complete arbitrariness. The idea of the creator of the moral universe may be meaningful, but there can be only one such creator if chaos is to be avoided. There must be a hierarchy between aesthetic and moral values if art is not to become destructive.[77] If this is the case, art can indeed be helpful and ease the human condition, and Allen hardly doubts that his own works, perhaps because of their intelligent criticism of art, achieve this aim. Mickey in *Hannah and Her Sisters* is saved from his suicidal intentions, connected with his incapacity to find out whether God really exists, by the Marx Brothers' *Duck Soup,* which does not solve his theological problem but shows that it is not necessary to do so in order to enjoy life. The reason why *Shadows and Fog,* one of Allen's most poetic works, does not end with Kleinman's murder, as did his early drama *Death,*[78] is precisely this: opposed to the Kafkaesque world threatened by the irrational murderer and at least to the same degree by the police and the vigilantes wanting to capture him is the counterworld of the artists (and the prostitutes). When the murderer assails Kleinman, the great magician Armstead manages to trap him, even if he finally escapes. The artist can prevent one murder, but he cannot overcome evil forever. And even if art may alleviate the burden of being, we have to face the possibility that it can deprive us of reality, as in the final scene when Armstead makes Kleinman and himself disappear. But in *Shadows and Fog* art is not the only way out from evil. The redeeming deed of the night is Irmy's adoption of the child whose mother was murdered. As in Kurosawa's *Rashomon* (and, in a different form, in *Alice*), the final seal on truth is moral commitment toward an innocent human being.

Ethics for Allen is certainly higher than aesthetics. But is ethics the highest stage? For Allen it is clear that there can be no religious limitation of ethics à la Kierkegaard—if religion claims something that is against sound ethics, we have to be extremely cautious. Irmy is right when (after she finds the crying orphan) she asks for part of the money back that she gave to the dubious Catholic priest; and the short second text in "The Scrolls," about Abraham's attempted slaughter of Isaac,[79] is the most direct and funniest refutation of Kierkegaard's *Fear and Trembling*. However, there may be a religious view of the universe that does not add any new norm to the usual moral precepts but rather offers a global perspective that allows us to see morality as somehow in tune with the universe. From young Alvy's anxiety about the expansion of the universe to the physicist Lloyd's remarks in *September* about modern cosmology and its purported teachings about an end of the world, including human life, to Kleinman's and Irmy's discussion about the spooky nature of light from stars that no longer exist, Allen has repeatedly expressed the Pascalian feeling that the universe as described by modern physics is hostile to any attempt to find meaning in it. Nevertheless, there are persons who manage to be both moral and loving toward the world as it is. Even if the Woody persona is usually a moralist, his moralism smacks of protest: he wants to be moral despite his contempt for the world as it is. Only one avatar of the Woody persona is somehow more in harmony with the world: Danny Rose. Danny Rose knows that without the recognition of an objective morality human beings cannot live well, and even if he recognizes that his former protégés leave him without guilt when they have become successful, he praises guilt as the sign of acknowledgment of an objective morality. "It's important to feel guilty. Otherwise, you, you know, you're capable of terrible things. . . . I-I'm guilty all the time and I-I never did anything. You know? My, my, my rabbi, Rabbi Perlstein, used to say we're all guilty in the eyes of God." And when Tina asks him whether he believes in God, Danny answers: "No, no. But uh, I'm guilty over it."[80] The answer is funny because Danny hardly wants to reveal something about feelings he happens to carry with him as a result of an oppressive education—his concept of guilt is a normative one, so his remarks recall Moore's paradox. Danny is not a committed believer, but he lacks the self-righteousness that areligious moralists often have; he is able to say yes even to suffering, and he is finally even able to forgive. "You know, you know what my philosophy of life is? That it's important to have some laughs, no question about it, but you got to suffer a little, too. Because otherwise, you miss the whole point of life."[81]

Danny is the closest the Woody persona can get to God. In *Crimes and Misdemeanors,* the director Allen introduces with Rabbi Ben a man who unites morality and religion in an admirable way (and is the only connection between the two strands of the film, the tragic and the comic). However, he becomes blind, while Judah Rosenthal, the man who commits the crime of ordering the murder of his former lover, is his successful ophthalmologist. Allen said that he wanted to make the point that Ben does not see the world as it is, even if he has the greatest gift one can have, a profound and sincere religious faith—"it surpasses even earthly love between a man and a woman."[82] But an interpretation of an artwork is not bound by the intentions of its author, and one could argue that Ben's blindness is as little a confutation of his wisdom as Danny Rose's betrayal by his former clients.

Of course, Ben errs with regard to Judah, but he may be closer to truth as a whole than the realist cynic who is right on this single point. The question has often been discussed whether the final scene of the movie, in which Judah speaks with Cliff in terms that seem to suggest that he has overcome any feelings of anxiety, is nihilistic. The same question has been asked again by critics after *Match Point,* Allen's strongest film in a decade, in which the murderer, against all odds, manages to escape detection by the police and to become a successful member of the British upper class. *Match Point* is even more disturbing than *Crimes and Misdemeanors,* since the comic strand is missing and therefore also the Woody persona. But perhaps more than in any earlier film, *Match Point* must be seen as forming one literary universe with another movie—*Scoop.* The complementarity is enhanced by the fact that the same actress, Scarlet Johansson, plays once the real, once the intended victim, who in *Scoop* proves able to defeat her lover who tries to kill her (and has killed an earlier lover in a way reminiscent of the manner depicted in *Match Point*). That Sondra Pransky is more successful than Nola Rice has to do with the fact that she is not as alone as the latter; in the Woody persona Sid Waterman she has found an eccentric but benevolent father figure who is not at all sexually interested in her but treats her as the daughter he has always longed for. Sid is, after Danny, probably the most attractive of the Woody personas, and his presence shifts the equilibrium back from the bleak statement represented by Allen's *Match Point.*

Again, are the final scenes of *Crimes and Misdemeanors* and of *Match Point* nihilistic? They hardly are; for, as Danny would say, the lack of the feeling of guilt may be worse than the feeling of guilt, not only for society, but for the individual himself, who loses, with the capacity to suffer, also any relation to the moral dimension of life. Rather than God's physical punishment (which in Dostoevsky's *Crime and Punishment* is the beginning of grace for Raskolnikov), God's withdrawal may be the greater evil.[83] The central scene of the film is Judah's visit to the house where he spent his childhood. Memories of a seder with his family come up, of a debate between his pious father, Sol, and his Marxist Aunt May. Her point is that if Hitler had won the war, he would have defined what was moral and there would have been no possibility of challenging his definition. But she suggests more—that his power would have become right. Sol objects, but not with rational arguments, for he does not trust logic as a last criterion and would always prefer God to truth.

It is clear that Allen sides neither with May nor with Sol. For him, murder remains evil, even if it is backed up by all the power in the world. But he cannot commit the *sacrificium intellectus* and relinquish truth for the sake of God. However, where does the objectivity of morality come from? Can we defend it without recognizing that being is more than the series of natural and social facts? And is it possible to believe in an objective moral principle and at the same time deny it any causal power—as is the case with the ideal world of *The Purple Rose of Cairo*? The idea that perhaps it is reason that obliges us to recognize the objectivity of morality and that this recognition entails logically that the universe, despite all appearances, is somehow structured by a moral principle does not occur to the philosophizing individual Allen, even if it lingers in his works, which enjoy with regard to him an autonomy similar to what Tom enjoys with regard to Gil. Allen never really considers the

thesis that the world could not be a place for the manifesta-
tion of pure morality if the good were always, or in most
cases, successful, and that therefore the striking divergence
between Is and Ought may be necessary for moral reasons.
A cosmotheology based on ethicotheology is a position
never debated in his universe, which remains bound to the
premises of existentialism and according to which art and
morality are acts and decisions of the individual and nothing
else—even if Allen feels horror at the idea that Aunt May
might be right. But it is difficult to counter her position with
something substantial and more than subjective if one rejects completely the idea of a rational theology.

The Historical Place of Allen's Version of the Comical

Allen is a *poeta doctus*. His allusions to classics of film
and literature are innumerable—from Greek tragedy to
Shakespeare, Russian literature, and twentieth-century film.
However, Allen's type of comedy is markedly different from
the New Comedy that developed in Hellenism and through
Roman comedy influenced European comedies till the eigh-
teenth and nineteenth centuries. It is much closer to Aristophanes than to Menander, Plautus, and Terence. Why? The
main reason seems to me that both Aristophanes and Allen
are contemporaries of the dissolution of a religion that for
centuries had been the basis of their culture—Greek poly-
theism and Judaic-Christian monotheism respectively. Allen
makes fun of God with the same ease with which Aristophanes made jokes about the Greek gods, and both have
been allowed to do so because the intellectuals of their time
did or do something analogous. In times of ideological un-

certainty comedy may share the task of questioning, together with the philosophers, the basic convictions of the age. (Also Rabelais' comic novel stems from a time in which at least traditional scholasticism—if not Christianity in general—had lost its credibility.) Comedy becomes thus inevitably more philosophical. Making fun of the gods or of God does not mean that one has to accept the mainstream critical ideologies—Aristophanes and Allen are indeed as sarcastic about them as they are about their religion. Both are at their core moralists, and they feel threatened by a form of intellectualism that they regard as empty and subversive (Aristophanes perhaps even more than Allen).

The ideological tension explains the high degree of reflexivity of Aristophanes' and Allen's comedy. Both artists deal again and again with the function of art in society, and they parody the noncomic works of their time—whether with respect (toward Aeschylus or Curtiz) or with sarcastic irony (toward Euripides or films à la "Purple Rose of Cairo"). The works of both show a clear awareness that social reality is mediated by literature (and film) and therefore are not at all realistic but often break through the mimetic illusion (in Aristophanes' case in the *parabaseis*). The Old Comedy never was Aristotelean theater in Brecht's sense, and Allen builds on a tradition that in the last centuries has more and more taken leave of the idea of an illusionist theater that forbids any interaction between the public and the artwork's content. Obviously, the wealth of expressive forms we find in Allen is greater—for the film has formal possibilities denied to theater, and the treasure of artworks that may be parodied has increased remarkably in the course of 2,400 years.

The New Comedy circles around one subject—the marriage of two young persons against the resistance of the elder generation. This topic is a result of the depoliticization that occurred in Hellenism with the demise of democracy—"higher" themes became taboo for comedians. While Aristophanes is an eminently political author, one cannot say the same of Allen. Both Aristophanes and Allen show the negative consequences of utopias; but in *The Birds* Aristophanes combines political ideas and a festive mood in a way completely alien to Allen, who furthermore lacks the poetic access to nature with which Aristophanes was gifted. Nevertheless Allen's comedy shares one negative trait with Aristophanes—the formation of a marriage is no longer the main end of comedy. This has to do with the crisis of marriage and its replacement by more informal relationships, besides the fact that parental objections no longer have a legal foothold: the resistance to marriage now stems from within the couple, rarely from outside. Nevertheless, Allen is closer to the New than to the Old Comedy because his main subject is the search for a partner, however provisory, a quest that has become even more demanding and complicated with the development of the romantic ideal. The psychoanalytic elimination of restraints regarding sexual speech, which had been introduced by Christianity, explains why Allen is as obscene as Aristophanes, even if his sexual jokes are more deflationary and less vital.

It is hardly an accident that Allen's comic universe blossomed in the last third of the twentieth century in New York, the Athens of late modernity. It presupposes the crisis of monotheism in the Western masses as well as the sexual revolution and at the same time a certain nostalgia for the older world. The United States modernized more quickly and more profoundly than Europe, but religious traditions there still have a vitality unknown in Europe. Furthermore, the Jewish form of intellectuality, so monstrously decimated in Europe, survived in the United States and even thrived, confronted as it was with chances of success and at the same time with the necessity of a redefinition in order to avoid absorption through mainstream modernity. Allen, whose grandparents immigrated around the turn of the century from Russia and Austria, preserved the European heritage (probably being closer to Russian than to German-speaking culture, even if his real name is German, Allan Stewart Konigsberg), and much of the *vis comica* of the Woody persona stems from the problems encountered by a man rooted more profoundly than he would like to admit in traditional Jewish values when he tries to date Waspy girls or make a career in a secular world whose ultimate end is success. His very European excess of reflexivity paralyzes him on the vital level; but he makes with grace and force the anti-Bergsonian point that this speaks more against life than against reflexivity, a quality of which Allen's work as a whole can stand as a valorization.

Notes

1. Maurice Yacowar, *Loser Take All: The Comic Art of Woody Allen* (New York, 1991), 2.

2. Diane Jacobs, ". . . But We Need the Eggs," in *The Magic of Woody Allen* (New York, 1982), 3, distinguishes the Woody persona, Allen (Woody Allen the creator), and Mr. Allen, the famous and wealthy man.

3. At a time when *Bullets over Broadway* had not yet been made, Allen regarded *The Purple Rose of Cairo* as his best film (E. Lax, *Woody Allen* [New York, 1991], 371). I am indebted to Lax's biography for much information.

4. The aesthetic necessity of such autonomy became obvious to Allen after the alterations visited on his script for *What's New, Pussycat?*, the disaster of *Casino Royale* (which does not even have a principal director), and the changes made by the producer of *What's Up, Tiger Lily?*, whom Allen sued (he dropped the suit after the film's critical success). See *Woody Allen on Woody Allen*, ed. Stig Björkman (New York, 1995), 10–15.

5. A defense of auteurism with regard to Woody Allen can be found in R. A. Blake, *Woody Allen: Profane and Sacred* (Lanham, MD, 1995), 14–15.

6. See S. H. Lee, *Woody Allen's Angst: Philosophical Commentaries on His Serious Films* (Jefferson, NC, 1997).

7. D. H. Monro, *Argument of Laughter* (Melbourne, 1951), 254.

8. Thomas Hobbes, *Leviathan* (Harmondsworth, 1981), 125 (chap. 6): "*Sudden Glory*, is the passion which maketh those *Grimaces* called LAUGHTER; and is caused either by some sudden act of their own, that pleaseth them; or by the apprehension of some deformed thing in another, by comparison whereof they suddenly applaud themselves."

9. Charles Darwin, *The Expression of the Emotions in Man and Animals* (Chicago, 1965), 360.

10. Darwin, *Expression of the Emotions,* 198. The peculiar form of expression of the mental state correlated with laughter is, according to Darwin, due to the principle of antithesis: the face assumes an expression and utters sounds opposed to those correlated with a state of distress (205). Herbert Spencer's explanation in *The Physiology of Laughter* appeals to another principle, namely that of the discharge of nervous energy.

11. The many connections between food and sex in Allen's movies are a major point in the useful work by Douglas Brode, *Woody Allen: His Films and Career* (Secaucus, NJ, 1985).

12. My translation of Henri Bergson, *Le rire: Essai sur la signification du comique* (Paris, 1940), 150: "Le rire est, avant tout, une correction. Fait pour humilier, il doit donner à la personne qui en est l'objet une impression pénible. La société se venge par lui des libertés qu'on a prises avec elle." See also 157: "Il faut bien qu'il y ait dans la cause du comique quelque chose de légèrement attentatoire (et de *spécifiquement* attentatoire) à la vie sociale, puisque la société y répond par un geste qui a tout l'air d'une réaction défensive, par un geste qui fait légèrement peur."

13. Bergson, *Le rire,* 5.

14. Jack's remark in *Stardust Memories* that "comedy is hostility" is not off the mark but it neglects that comedy is both hostility and a taming of hostility.

15. It would be interesting to analyze the moral objections against laughter (which draw partly on the attack against authorities that laughter may represent, partly on some of the taboo objects experienced as funny, and partly on the feeling of superiority of the laugher). Those objections played a certain role in the Middle Ages; they have become popular through Jorge of Burgos in Umberto Eco's *Name of the Rose,* but even in a work as recent as Thomas Mann's *Doctor Faustus* laughter is seen as highly ambivalent. See Mark Roche, "Laughter and Truth in *Doktor Faustus,*" *Deutsche Vierteljahrsschrift für Literaturwissenschaft und Geistesgeschichte* 60 (1986): 309–32. A good recent discussion of the issue can be found in Berys Gaut, "Just Joking: The Ethics and Aesthetics of Humor," *Philosophy and Literature* 22, no. 1 (1998): 51–68,

as well as in Francis H. Buckley, *The Morality of Laughter* (Ann Arbor, 2003).

16. See Mary P. Nichols, *Reconstructing Woody* (Lanham, MD, 1998), 212: "In the best case, those laughing at the stand-up comic are also laughing at themselves."

17. See Darwin, *Expression of the Emotions,* 206.

18. See Paul Ekman and Wallace V. Friesen, *Unmasking the Face* (Englewood Cliffs, NJ, 1975), 101–2.

19. The difference plays an important role in Jean Paul's *Vorschule der Asthetik* (see esp. § 29 of the second edition of 1813), in Georg Wilhelm Friedrich Hegel's *Vorlesungen über die Ästhetik,* 20 vols., Theorie-Werkausgabe (Frankfurt, 1969), 15:527–28, and in Northrop Frye, *Anatomy of Criticism* (Princeton, 1957), who places comedy proper between romance on the one hand and irony and satire on the other.

20. The distinction can be traced back to Plato *Symposium* 189b. A rudimentary theory of comedy can be found in his *Philebus* 48a–50b.

21. Arthur Schopenhauer, *Die Welt als Wille und Vorstellung,* 1.13 and 2.8. The distinction between conceptual and verbal witticism goes back at least to Cicero (*On the Orator* 2.59.240), who influenced the long treatment of humor at the end of the second book of Baldassare Castiglione's *The Courtier.*

22. See Arthur Schopenhauer, *Zürcher Ausgabe,* 10 vols. (Zurich, 1977), 3:118: "diese strenge, unermüdliche, überlästige Hofmeisterin Vernunft jetzt ein Mal der Unzulänglichkeit überführt zu sehn, muß uns daher ergötzlich sein."

23. Plato *Hippias major* 287e3f.

24. Munro, *Argument of Laughter,* 157.

25. I have in mind the *Tractatus Coislinianus.* See Lane Cooper, *An Aristotelian Theory of Comedy* (New York, 1922), 225 and 239ff.

26. Woody Allen, *Four Films of Woody Allen* (London, 1983), 197.

27. Woody Allen, *Side Effects* (New York, 1975), 53, 42.

28. "Retribution" is the title of a short story that plays with inversion (Allen, *Side Effects,* 131–49). Of course, repetition and inversion can be combined, as in the iterated phone calls by Deborah Fifer in *Scenes from a Mall,* which cancel and reestablish, cancel and reestablish

the dinner invitation, the repetition being caused by an inversion of the couple's behavior.

29. Cf. Mark Roche's concept of "comedy of withdrawal" in his magisterial work *Tragedy and Comedy* (Albany, 1998), 175ff. I owe much to this extraordinary study, which combines great conceptual clarity with a most impressive command of world literature.

30. Monro, *Argument of Laughter*, 134–35.

31. Recall Kant's famous definition of laughter as "an affection arising from the sudden transformation of a strained expectation into nothing" ("ein Affekt aus der plötzlichen Verwandlung einer gespannten Erwartung in nichts," *Kritik der Urteilskraft*, B 225).

32. Aristotle *Poetics* 1449a33f. See also Cicero *On the Orator* 2.59.238.

33. *Failures* at killing, as in *Take the Money and Run* (and a fortiori at suicide, such as Maxwell's in *A Midsummer Night's Sex Comedy* or Mickey's in *Hannah and Her Sisters*), may be funny as in Oscar Wilde's *Lord Arthur Savile's Crime: A Study in Duty*, where the comic effect is increased by the hero's conviction, sharply contrasting with our usual norms, that he has a duty to commit the murder predicted.

34. Bergson, *Le rire*, 110. Hegel, who may not share Bergson's interpretation of the main character and in any case strictly distinguishes between the comic and the satiric, does not consider *Tartuffe* funny (*Vorlesungen über die Ästhetik*, 15:570).

35. Cf. Roche, *Tragedy and Comedy*, 212ff. In Albert Bermel, *Farce: A History from Aristophanes to Woody Allen* (New York, 1982), danger, destruction, and torment are regarded as moments of farce.

36. Sigmund Freud, *Jokes and Their Relation to the Unconscious* (London, 1966), 101.

37. Allen, *Four Films*, 140.

38. Woody Allen, *Side Effects*, 123–29, and *Getting Even* (London, 1975), 35–40.

39. Furthermore, in his short texts parody plays an important role, whether the parody is of Ibsen or of Vincent and Theo van Gogh's letters ("Lovborg's Women Considered" and "If the Impressionists Had Been Dentists," in *Without Feathers* [New York, 1972], 26–31 and 188–93, respectively).

40. Allen, *Getting Even*, 33.

41. Allen, *Four Films*, 328.

42. Allen, *Getting Even*, 60–61.

43. Allen, *Side Effects*, 99–111, 110.

44. Woody Allen, *Hannah and Her Sisters* (New York, 1987), 109.

45. W. J. Fuchs, *Die vielen Gesichter des Woody Allen* (Cologne, 1986), 10ff., compares the Woody persona with Donald Duck but neglects the ambivalent nature of Woody's failure.

46. Nichols, *Reconstructing Woody*, 28ff.

47. In *Stardust Memories,* Sandy insists that *The Bicycle Thief* is much deeper than a social problem: "There's so many wonderful ambiguities in it. It's much more profound than that" (Allen, *Four Films,* 350).

48. "Accanto metterei, proprio al vertice, *La grande illusione* e *Ladri di biciclette,*" *La Repubblica,* August 14, 1987, 19.

49. In *Stardust Memories* Sandy is torn between the warm mother Isobel and, as she rightly says, "those dark woman with all their problems"—"they give you a hard time and you like it" (Allen, *Four Films,* 375).

50. Foster Hirsch, *Love, Sex, Death, and the Meaning of Life: Woody Allen's Comedy* (New York, 1981), 3–4.

51. Woody Allen, *Three Films of Woody Allen* (New York, 1987), 250.

52. See Vittorio Hösle, *Morals and Politics* (Notre Dame, 2004), 353–54. The feminist critique of Woody Allen usually overlooks this point, even if there may be some wishful thinking in Allen's construction of women and their love for the Woody persona.

53. Allen, *Side Effects,* 78.

54. Allen, *Four Films,* 338.

55. Björkman, *Woody Allen on Woody Allen*, 86.

56. Björkman, *Woody Allen on Woody Allen,* 211.

57. An analogous joke can be found in "The Condemned" (Allen, *Side Effects,* 9–16, 12), which contains many of the ideas of *Love and Death* but ends with the acquittal of the person condemned for a murder he considered but did not perpetrate.

58. Allen, *Three Films,* 223.

59. Lax, *Woody Allen,* 276.

60. Allen, *Three Films,* 40.

61. Allen, *Three Films,* 68.

62. Allen, *Three Films,* 76.

63. Allen, *Three Films,* 115.

64. Allen, *Three Films,* 214.

65. Allen, *Hannah and Her Sisters,* 133.

66. Allen, *Getting Even,* 139–51.

67. Allen, *Without Feathers,* 123–79.

68. Allen, *Without Feathers,* 177.

69. Sandy Bates in *Stardust Memories* (Allen, *Four Films,* 334–35).

70. This may disappoint (see S. Kauffmann's review "A Midwinter Night's Dream," now in *Perspectives on Woody Allen,* ed. R. R. Curry [New York, 1996], 37–40). But it is what Allen wants to say, and he says it well. It may furthermore console Allen's critics to know that his opinion about film criticism is even bleaker than that about art.

71. Allen, *Three Films,* 333.

72. Allen, *Three Films,* 395.

73. Allen, *Three Films,* 404.

74. Allen, *Three Films,* 408.

75. Arnold W. Preussner, "Woody Allen's *The Purple Rose of Cairo* and the Genres of Comedy," in Curry, *Perspectives on Woody Allen,* 91.

76. Allen, *Four Films,* 124.

77. See Hösle, *Morals and Politics,* 79.

78. Allen, *Without Feathers,* 39–100.

79. Allen, *Without Feathers,* 23–24.

80. Allen, *Three Films,* 224.

81. Allen, *Three Films,* 254.

82. Björkman, *Woody Allen on Woody Allen,* 223.

83. Cf. Mark Roche, "Justice and the Withdrawal of God in Woody Allen's *Crimes and Misdemeanors,*" *Journal of Value Inquiry* 29 (1995): 547–63.

Index of Films by Woody Allen